In Praise of *Peak Business Performance Under Pressure*

"Maybe once in a lifetime you meet an individual who possesses the uniquely rare combined skills of honor, integrity, respect, vision, wisdom, deft reaction, and a singular focus of excellence under extreme pressure. Driscoll's accomplishments in the field of battle are legendary, and his accomplishments as an outstanding human being, business leader, and visionary are equally impressive. *Peak Business Performance Under Pressure* is so compelling for all these reasons, and because it translates feats of almost unimaginable air battle into day-to-day tools for winning in the rough, new flat business world today. Kudos for such unparalleled excellence!"

> — Joel Marcus, Chairman, Chief Executive Officer, and
> Founder, Alexandria Real Estate Equities, Inc.

"Priceless advice for senior executives and leaders! Having had the rare personal pleasure of seeking Bill Driscoll's counsel as a senior military officer, and now striving to excel as a new president/CEO within the private sector, I can attest to the relevance of *Peak Business Performance Under Pressure*. This is the must-read for today's business leaders who seek to leverage the very best of our nation's lessons learned and heroic past."

> — Robert F. Willard, Admiral, U.S. Navy (Ret.); former
> Commander, U.S. Pacific Fleet; President and CEO,
> Institute of Nuclear Power Operations

"A world-class book from one of Naval Aviation's greatest heroes. *Peak Business Performance Under Pressure* is a compelling, historical, inspirational, and extremely relevant read for an audience of CEOs and business leaders facing the economic challenges of today's world."

> — Mike McCabe, former Commander, U.S. Third Fleet

"What a great book, written by an American hero. *Peak Business Performance Under Pressure* gives you the detailed plans and disciplines needed to be successful and ready for the challenges of the global business world we live in today. It is now required reading for all leaders at Datron. Thank you, Bill, for helping prepare leaders for the 'dogfights' ahead, and for your heart of service in helping others grow."

> — Art Barter, President and CEO, Datron World
> Communications, Inc.

"Exquisitely researched, toned by Willy Driscoll's personal air combat experience, and impeccably true to what spelled success for many of the greatest heroes of the modern era. An unprecedented work, *Peak Business Performance Under Pressure* should be on the reading list of every CEO in America."

> — Lyle Bien, Admiral, U.S. Navy (Ret.); Strategic Adviser in the Aerospace Industry

"Bill Driscoll has transitioned the principles from TOPGUN—an elite training operation where results are measured in the survival or death of their customers—to the management and sales world. His approach will change your thinking and increase your bottom-line impact. I challenge you to lay the book down before you read the last page!"

> — Dan McKinnon, President and CEO Emeritus, North American Airlines; former Chairman, U.S. Civil Aeronautics Board

"*Peak Business Performance Under Pressure* lays out a methodical flight path to achieve self-discipline, laser focus, and the skills to successfully roll, bank, and dive through the daily dogfights in business today. This book has both guns blazing, yet Driscoll inspires with a touchingly simple appreciation of life and with a moral strength that only one who has pushed the odds of survival to the limit can do."

> — Greg Geraci, Senior Vice President, CBRE

"In *Peak Business Performance Under Pressure*, I recognize some of the disciplines I use as a business executive with Northrop Grumman Corporation. This book takes those disciplines to a new level and is a must-have for all business executives operating in a pressure-packed corporate environment."

> — JJ Quinn, Rear Admiral, U.S. Navy (Ret.); Vice President, Northrop Grumman Corporation

"This book provides the unique perspective of applying the disciplined, rigorous methods used so successfully by the best instructors and winners in air combat to the daily process of succeeding in business. A comprehensive blend of establishing and sharpening personal habits with physical, mental, and emotional optimization, it provides a solid game plan for those looking to step up their game. Whether early in your business career or in the C-suite, *Peak Business Performance Under Pressure* will provide you with a compelling, fresh, and proven perspective on how to win life's game."

— Dan Donoghue, Commander, U.S. Navy (Ret.); former Senior Vice President, Whitley, Bradley & Brown Consulting

"Proven, practical techniques and behaviors that *will* improve your performance when you need it most. A must-read for the serious leader."

— Alan Mullen, Chairman and Founder, Crew Training International, Inc.

"Bill Driscoll has come up with an extraordinary way of comparing how top military pilots handle the pressures of aerial combat and everyday demands facing today's businessmen and women. The result is a breathtaking ride in his F-4 Phantom that will have you on the edge of your seat while at the same time providing solid advice as to how to succeed in business."

— Robert P. Hickey, Rear Admiral, U.S. Navy (Ret.); former COO of Gardner Industries

"A must for anyone who wants to better understand what it takes to succeed in business and in life. Learn from the Aces and apply the principles to your daily work. Their system is brilliant and proven!"

— Dennis J. Carlo, Biotechnology Pioneer; President and CEO, Adamis Pharmaceuticals Corporation

"*Peak Business Performance Under Pressure* is a must-read for anyone who aspires to accomplish great things while leading a full life. Driscoll's broad experiences, combined with strong family and community values, provide a unique perspective on how we can sustain a dedication to achieving both excellence and balance."

— Kevin J. Danehy, Executive Vice President, CBRE

"We are not born with the skills needed to succeed in today's competitive business environment . . . but they *can* be studied and developed. In *Peak Business Performance Under Pressure*, Bill Driscoll captures the lessons learned by pilots who have succeeded at the highest level in one of the most competitive environments of all—combat aviation—and shares the invaluable strategies with those who are serious about winning in the intense arena of modern business."

— Dave Frost, President, Frost and Associates

PEAK BUSINESS PERFORMANCE UNDER PRESSURE

A Navy Ace Shows
How to Make Great Decisions
in the Heat of Business Battles

BILL DRISCOLL

WITH PETER JOFFRE NYE

FOREWORD BY SENATOR JOHN MCCAIN

ALLWORTH PRESS
NEW YORK

Allworth Press books may be purchased in bulk at special discounts for sales
promotion, corporate gifts, fund-raising, or educational purposes. Special
editions can also be created to specifications. For details, contact the Special Sales
Department, Allworth Press, 307 West 36th Street, 11th Floor, New York, NY 10018
or info@skyhorsepublishing.com.

21 20 19 18   5 4 3

Published by Allworth Press, an imprint of Skyhorse Publishing, Inc.
307 West 36th Street, 11th Floor, New York, NY 10018.

Allworth Press® is a registered trademark of Skyhorse Publishing, Inc.®, a Delaware
corporation.

www.allworth.com

Cover and interior design by Rian Anderson
Cover image: Original painting by Philip E. West. Image published by Military
Gallery—A Division of Griffon International PLC.

Library of Congress Cataloging-in-Publication Data is available on file.

Print ISBN: 978-1-62153-424-2
Ebook ISBN: 978-1-62153-421-1

Printed in the United States of America

This book is dedicated to all the men and women who've ever served in our country's Armed Forces and their families. Thanks to you, we continue to be "the land of the free" because we are also "the home of the brave."

Acknowledgments

Writing *Peak Business Performance Under Pressure* turned out to be a very interesting challenge. Many exceptional people from a wide variety of backgrounds provided invaluable insight, suggestions, and advice. First, I owe a huge debt of gratitude to my co-author, Peter Nye. We faced a tough assignment: how to put the combat lessons of Ace fighter pilots into appropriate business context. I thoroughly enjoyed our weekly phone calls over a period of almost fifteen months while putting the initial draft of the manuscript together.

Since we made repeated reference to what I had learned as a TOPGUN instructor, we needed to make sure our business ideas, concepts, and guidelines were consistent with key elements of TOPGUN training. We therefore sought the advice of several former TOPGUN instructors who later became highly successful business leaders. We'd like to extend a special thanks to former TOPGUN instructors John (Woody) Forester of Federal Express; Al (Shoes) Mullen, also of Federal Express and founder, former CEO/president of Crew Training International; Mike (Wizard) McCabe, former Commander of the Third Fleet and CEO of Ryan International Airlines; and Lyle (Ho Chi) Bien, retired three-star admiral and strategic adviser in the aerospace industry.

We also needed to make sure our leadership principles of aircraft carrier commanding officers presented an accurate picture of that job. We got invaluable insight from the following aircraft carrier commanding officers: Bob (Burner) Hickey of the USS *Ranger*, retired two-star admiral and former COO of Gardner Industries; JJ Quinn of the USS *Abraham Lincoln*, retired one-star admiral, former TOPGUN instructor, and Vice President of Business Development with Northrop Grumman; Dave (Falcon) Frost of the USS *Saratoga*, retired three-star admiral, former commanding officer of TOPGUN, and President of Frost & Associates.

We then had to blend all of this great information into a workable format for today's mid- to upper-level executives serious about taking their performance to the next level. We owe a huge debt of gratitude to the following business leaders: Art Barter, President and CEO of Datron World Communications; Dennis Carlo, President and CEO of Adamis Pharmaceuticals; Joel Marcus, President and CEO of Alexandria Real Estate Equities; Bob Willard, President and CEO of the Institute of Nuclear Power Operations, recently retired four-star admiral and commander of the Pacific Fleet, former commanding officer of the aircraft carrier USS *Abraham Lincoln*, and former TOPGUN instructor; Dan McKinnon, former cabinet member for President Ronald Reagan, Chairman of the Civil Aeronautics Board, and CEO Emeritus of North American Airlines; Robert Marzano, President and CEO, Marzano Research Laboratory; Greg Geraci, Senior Vice President of CBRE; Dan Donoghue, former Senior Vice President with Whitley, Bradley & Brown; Bernie Gilmore, Senior Vice President of Industrial Development for Mitsui Fudosan in Southern California; Kevin Danehy, Executive Vice President of CBRE; Ted Owen, President of the Carlsbad Chamber of Commerce and former Editor of the *San Diego Business Journal*; and Mike Rioux, Chief Operating Officer of JDA Aviation Technology Solutions.

All this powerful information and valuable lessons of top performers were brought to life thanks to the exceptional organizational skills of developmental editor Lorna Gentry. Our publisher, Robb Clouse, offered us constant encouragement and sage advice throughout this whole process. His staff, spearheaded by Vice President of Marketing Gretchen Knapp, Editorial Director Lesley Bolton, and Executive Assistant David Gray, provided great wisdom and encouragement.

Our new publisher, Skyhorse Publishing, Inc., continues that commitment to excellence which has been so important to us. We are grateful for the wisdom of Allworth Publisher Tad Crawford, the thorough support of Skyhorse Publisher Tony Lyons, the marketing insight of Bill Wolfsthal, Director of Sales and Marketing, the steady guidance of Editorial Assistant Zoe Wright, and the coordination with national book outlets by Kathryn Mennone, Director of Special Markets.

We'd also like to thank those twenty-six Ace fighter pilots and their families for their time and remarkable lessons of air combat. The more than 200 senior executives we interviewed helped to keep us focused on those lessons of greatest value for today's executives who are serious about learning how to perform at their best when the pressure on them is the greatest.

Bill Driscoll
Centerville, Massachusetts
July 2014

Table of Contents

Foreword

It is a rare occasion when an attack pilot praises the lessons of any member of the fighter community; however Vietnam Ace Bill "Willie" Driscoll is more than worthy of our respect and admiration. Those that can claim the title of "Fighter Ace" belong to an elite club and Bill's victories in Vietnam were legend then, and remain so today.

His military resume includes over 170 combat missions and four years as a flight instructor at TOPGUN, Naval Aviation's post-graduate school in air-to-air fighter tactics. His civilian resume as a top performer in the field of commercial real estate for over 26 years is nearly as impressive.

In *Peak Business Performance Under Pressure*, Bill blends his military and civilian experiences, translating military victory into business successes. Backed up by extensive interviews with successful business executives, and his own personal experiences Bill has identified specific work habits and leadership skills that are essential to executive success.

All pilots know well the only rule in a dogfight: there are no rules. In *Peak Business Performance Under Pressure*, Bill allows readers a look inside the cockpit during his combat dogfights and offers a revealing set of guidelines for professional and personal success from one of the country's finest fighter Aces.

—Senator John McCain

Introduction

It was May 10, 1972, and I was flying my 170th and final combat mission over North Vietnam as the Radar Intercept Officer in a two-seat U.S. Navy F-4 Phantom jet fighter. The pilot, Randy (Duke) Cunningham, and I were providing fighter cover for eighteen nearly defenseless Navy attack aircraft near the Gulf of Tonkin. We were a solid team with two enemy shoot-downs on our service record. But that day, when our flight was jumped by about twenty-five enemy MIG jet fighters, every moment of our training and experience was put to the ultimate test. We were about to engage in what would become the Vietnam War's largest air battle, during which we would learn, firsthand, the critical demands of decision making under some of the most stressful and demanding conditions we could have imagined.

Within seconds of entering the enemy's airspace, we were attacked. At speeds topping 600 mph, we twisted our jet wildly in a series of evasive maneuvers, dipping sharply toward the ground as we dodged an onslaught of surface-to-air missiles and anti-aircraft artillery. Suddenly, the shooting stopped. Within seconds, the deafening quiet was shattered again as a swarm of enemy jet fighters raced toward us. We quickly rolled in and shot down two of the enemy planes before they could attack our unsuspecting teammates. Then, we saw another enemy jet—this one making a head-on gun attack at our F-4 Phantom.

Now we were in a dogfight, pitted against the enemy's leading Ace, an international designation for military aviators who shoot down at least five enemy planes in aerial combat. With our bodies struggling against crushing G-force pressures, at times equivalent to 1,400 pounds, we remained locked in battle for nearly two minutes— an eternity for supersonic jet fighters. Our enemy had us in his gun sight the entire time, unleashing withering blasts of machine gun fire at our most vulnerable times. And then, in an instant, he made one catastrophic error. We immediately pounced on him and won.

The skies grew quiet. We quickly realized the other aircraft in our flight had been widely scattered, leaving us alone, forty miles inside enemy territory. As we started our climb to leave, we felt totally drained. We were drenched in a cold, clammy sweat, our throats raw from gulping oxygen through our tight-fitting masks and our mouths filled with the metallic taste of fear. Waves of nausea from the strain of that vicious two-minute dogfight swept over us, and our limbs stiffened from the effects of those extremely high G-forces. In just five minutes, we had shot down three enemy jets. Now we were Aces, we were alive, and our final mission was nearly over.

I gave Duke a "safe" heading home to our aircraft carrier, the USS *Constellation*, on station about 100 miles offshore in the South China Sea. Gaining altitude, we saw the emerald-green ocean glistening peacefully in the distance. Our plan was to climb to 29,000 feet and reduce airspeed to save fuel during what we thought would be an uneventful flight back to the ship. Jubilant with relief and joy, Duke and I exchanged a rapid back-and-forth replay of the dogfights through our inter-cockpit radio. We sighted two additional enemy jet fighters circling the treetops well below us, but we paid them little attention. Relaxing our normally razor-sharp focus, we celebrated our victories.

It was a big—almost fatal—mistake. Without warning, we were blinded by a brilliant white flash followed by a thunderous explosion that immediately snapped us back to attention. Our eighteen-ton jet convulsed, shuddered, and rolled as what sounded like a hail storm of iron pellets slammed into its belly. We banked right to see that, under our wing, a bright orange fire-cloud was blossoming from the end of a jagged white smoke trail extending up from the treetops below.

We had been hit by a surface-to-air missile (SAM) the size of a telephone pole and carrying more than 400 pounds of high explosives. The SAM had closed on us, at a speed of a half-mile per second, the equivalent of ten football fields. We never saw it coming.

For about thirty seconds, our Phantom seemed to fly normally, and I thought we had made a narrow escape. Then, our wounded plane rolled sideways in a lazy skid, losing one of the main hydraulic systems that powered its flight controls. Within seconds, the other hydraulic system started to fail. Without it, we would lose our flight controls system and be forced to eject immediately. We knew if we could only stay airborne for about three more minutes, we might reach the ocean, where we'd stand a better chance for rescue by Navy helicopters—and maybe avoid being captured and tortured as prisoners of war. In a lightning-fast decision made under extreme pressure, we decided to stay with our crippled jet a little longer.

We were still fifteen miles inside enemy airspace. Our jet was on fire, smoke and flames creeping into the cockpit. Strapped tightly into my ejection seat, I strained to shift my body away from the licking flames. Meanwhile, those two enemy MIGs had climbed to our altitude and were closing in to finish us. Now we had to make another rapid, life-or-death decision. In our training, we had learned of another pilot's experience with the same type of SAM hit, in which he had controlled his crippled plane's direction using only the rudders. We knew this technique would make our flight extremely unpredictable, but it was our only hope. We decided to go for it.

As our plane spiraled downward, our tension, anxiety, and stress soared to stratospheric heights, but Duke's remarkable piloting skills never wavered. We narrowly avoided losing complete control of our F-4 Phantom at the top of three different vertical loops as we barrel-rolled toward the sea. Just as we approached the coastline, our plane abruptly skidded sideways, then started spinning violently out of control. Seconds later, it snap-rolled upside down, slamming us against the domes of our canopies. We were now totally out of control in an inverted spin, pinned by the incredible force of our downward spiral in cockpits engulfed in fire and smoke.

It was my job to somehow get us both out alive. I groped for the ejection handle mounted on my seat, but against the force of the plane's spinning, rolling negative Gs, my reach was too short. In a last desperate move, I pressed my left hand against the top of the canopy and, in an adrenaline-fueled burst of strength, raised my twisted body in a one-armed handstand. It worked. I was able to curl the top third of the first two fingers of my right hand around the ejection handle and pull.

By the clock, about three-quarters of a second passed in complete silence. Then came an explosion that rocketed us out of our cockpits and threw us somersaulting through the air. I was so pumped on adrenaline that I hardly felt the 180 mph windblast of my ejection. With a rapid-tumble view alternating between the pale blue sky and the emerald sea, I plummeted downward, still strapped in my 200-pound ejection seat. Then I felt a sharp jerk—my parachute had opened and I separated from the ejection seat. Our fiery, smoking Phantom spiraled into the South China Sea like a burning, wind-blown leaf as we floated down at about 110 feet per second over the mouth of the enemy's main harbor.

Now my survival training took over. While still in my descent, I pulled out my emergency radio and broadcast our position to Navy rescue personnel. I also transmitted the location of some fast-moving enemy patrol boats racing through the water toward us.

I tried not to look at the survival raft that dangled from a forty-foot nylon line connected to my survival gear. As my training had taught me, I kept my eyes fixed on the horizon until the raft hit the water. Less than a second later, I was in the water. I carefully shed my parachute and swam away from it before it could drag me to the ocean floor. I then crawled into the inflated raft, pulled out my survival pistol, checked that it was loaded, and prepared for a possible shoot-out. About a half-mile away, Duke had landed and gone through the same procedure. We didn't know the fate of those enemy PT boats and prepared for yet another attack.

But none came. U.S. Navy attack aircraft had responded immediately to my broadcast, sinking the enemy patrol boats. About twenty minutes later, Navy helicopters came to our rescue.

We were exhausted, exhilarated, and amazed—proud of our training, humbled by our experience, and grateful for the outcome. Our shoot-down of three MIGs would make us the only Navy Aces to come out of the Vietnam War. But we had been shot down by a SAM and barely avoided a violent death by fire—a horrific event that we could have prevented. By allowing our focus to waver, we almost lost our lives. Fortunately, our training and preparation had equipped us to make the essential split-second decisions and to call upon the peak performance skills necessary to survive in spite of that momentary lapse.

Winning the Dogfight of Global Business

So how does this all relate to you? As a busy executive, team leader, or decision maker, you may think you have little in common with Ace fighter pilots. After all, their single, overriding mission is to fly into enemy territory, dodge a barrage of exploding flak, find enemy aircraft, and shoot them down, no matter what. As the Red Baron, Manfred von Richthofen, once famously said on this subject, "All else is rubbish." But today's businesses are engaged in their own dogfights and unrelenting calls to combat. To survive in the extremely fast-paced, competitive battleground of global enterprise, business leaders must be able to handle big, rapidly changing problems; make critical decisions under intense pressure; build strong, committed teams; maintain unwavering focus on their missions; and—always—demonstrate the credibility and loyalty they expect from others. Meeting those demands is a tough job, and not everyone can do it.

In any dogfight, only the best-prepared will win. Aces make up less than 4 percent of all fighter pilots who ever flew against enemy planes, yet they account for greater than 40 percent of enemy airplane shoot-downs. What are their secrets? What do they do differently than other fighter pilots? And how can their battle-tested formula translate to the competitive arena of global enterprise? In this book, you're going to learn the answers to these questions. We'll examine the winning leadership and decision-making techniques of Ace fighter pilots and how the lessons of air combat can help you achieve peak performance under pressure to become a stronger, more effective leader in your office, team, or organization.

As you are about to learn, much of what flying Aces do so well under pressure demands some of the same skills and training you need to perform your best at work. The ideas and techniques you learn in this book will prepare you to cope with the battleground conditions every business leader faces today—never-ending tight deadlines and ever-higher expectations, dwindling resources and unexpected company acquisitions, constant downsizing and rightsizing, and sudden upheavals in management.

For executives, as for fighter pilots, failure is not an option. To survive, you need to have a rock-solid plan in place to handle ever-present challenges. In this book, I'll outline the Aces' concrete formula for creating and managing just such a plan, so you can perform at your best when nothing short of your best will do. Here, you'll find easy-to-implement guidelines for identifying and dealing with your biggest sources of workplace stress, including how to create and implement the most effective plans, how to prepare yourself mentally and physically for peak performance, how to build do-or-die collaborative teams, how to assess your strengths and weaknesses and use them to outgun your competition, how to build credibility with colleagues and clients, and how to adopt a lifelong training program to maintain your skills as a "business Ace." Together, these techniques form the kind of TOPGUN-style training that will help you elevate your performance to the highest levels. In the process, you will learn to live a more productive, balanced, and happy life, despite the ever-expanding competition and increasing pressures that confront every decision maker in today's workplace.

Acing the Formula: What's in It for You?

You probably picked up this book because you're facing a number of critical questions related to your future, as well as the future of your business or industry. Is there such a thing today as a long-term customer? A guaranteed job? How can you win on the shifting battleground of your marketplace? In our digital age and expanding global economy, more people than ever may have a need for your goods and services, but the competition today comes from everywhere—and out of nowhere. Your competitors want what you have, and they'll do just about anything to steal your clients. Are you fending off these attacks? And are you expanding and growing your customer base? Will your company survive—can *you* survive?

These are the types of questions that have compelled countless organizations and executives to turn to the TOPGUN-style training techniques I offer in my seminars and in individual and organizational consultation—the same combat-proven approach you are about to learn. Here, you will find tools, techniques, and guidelines that will help you overcome any issues or unanswered questions that may be holding you back from your own peak performance. Whether you need to become more productive right away, improve your ability to hire and retain the right people, structure better teams, or lead them more effectively, the answers you're looking for are all related—and we will examine each of them in the chapters ahead.

The leadership tools and techniques I have outlined in this book aren't based solely on my experiences as a Navy Ace. They also draw on skills and tactics I learned as a four-year TOPGUN instructor and twenty-four-year air-combat consultant for TOPGUN, as well as during my twenty-six years as a leading commercial real estate salesman. For the past seventeen years, as a consultant to some of the most successful companies in the United States, I have been training decision makers at every organizational level to leverage the same skills, techniques, and processes I have laid out for you in this book—all contained in the six elements of a simple but powerful formula for winning under even the most high-pressure conditions:

PLANNING + PREPARATION +
FOCUS + ASSESSMENT +   =   PEAK
IMPROVEMENT + SELF-DISCIPLINE   PERFORMANCE

To illustrate the real-world application of that formula, I have supplemented my own observations and experiences with those drawn from my interviews with twenty-six of the 150 Aces living in the United States today and more than 200 senior-executive leaders from a broad range of businesses and industries. Here's what you will learn about leveraging the techniques of this powerful formula:

- Chapter 1 outlines each of the six elements in the Peak Performance Formula, how that formula enables Ace fighter pilots to win no matter what, and how their methods can work for you. This chapter's assessment enables you to quickly identify your own peak performance challenges.

- In chapter 2, you learn essential techniques for creating winning plans, including a targeted overview of the three must-have elements in any

ABOUT TOPGUN

During the first half of the Vietnam War, Navy fighter pilots performed poorly in air combat—much more poorly than in previous conflicts. For every two enemy airplanes the Navy shot down, it lost one of its own. The Navy determined that its fighter pilot training program was to blame for this stinging 2:1 "exchange" ratio. Following the advent of sophisticated radar systems and air-to-air missiles, the Navy deemphasized training its fighter pilots in dogfighting, believing that kind of close-range air combat had become obsolete. They were wrong! To rebuild its strong dogfighting skills, the Navy established the United States Navy Fighter Weapons School, popularly known as TOPGUN, in 1969.

The Navy still had a small group of fighter pilots who were highly skilled at flying their jets to the absolute limit and winning these dogfights. That group became the first TOPGUN instructors, and they succeeded at setting up the finest postgraduate-level dogfight training squadron in the world. As a result of TOPGUN training, the Navy's exchange ratio for the remainder of the Vietnam War jumped to an astounding 33:1. TOPGUN still exists today, more than forty years after its inception, and graduates four classes each year. The Navy selects only the best aviators to attend TOPGUN, and its instructors continue to be the finest aviators in the world—all former TOPGUN graduates whose performances as students distinguished them as "the best of the best."

successful business plan, and a logical four-step approach to using your personal daily action plan to accomplish your strategic, operational, and tactical goals.

- Chapter 3 outlines some concrete steps for mastering the five levels of essential preparation for both team and personal success—and for building the kind of physical, emotional, and psychological readiness that will help you overcome your biggest challenges and toughest competition—in any arena.

- Chapter 4 takes a close look at the Aces' techniques for developing and maintaining laser-beam focus and attention to detail, and it offers a simple, three-step process for adopting those techniques to boost personal and team performance.

- In chapter 5, you learn why ongoing assessment is essential to attaining peak performance, some easy-to-follow methods for assessing your performance and that of your team, and how to infuse your organization with the kind of essential accountability necessary to establish standards of excellence, gain customer trust, and improve outcomes in every aspect of the operation.

- Chapter 6 offers specific tools and techniques for making ongoing improvements in your personal, team, and organizational performance. From improving self-discipline to acing key leadership skills, building confidence, and expanding your sphere of influence, the skills you learn in this chapter help you become a more effective decision maker, in any environment and under any level of pressure.

- Chapter 7 pulls together your "training program," as it outlines how your ability to consistently adhere to the Peak Performance Formula enables you to face some of the most common workplace ambushes and respond expertly to any rapidly evolving challenge. Here, you learn some simple principles for integrating the ideas and practices you've gained in the book into a never-fail plan for surviving and thriving—both personally and professionally.

Winning—Every Time

Before we get started, I want to make one thing very clear: there is nothing glamorous or cool about an actual combat dogfight. A jet fighter plane is a sleek piece of machinery that lends a false sense of dignity to what is nothing more than a vicious, violent, gladiator-like brawl to the death. The dogfight has only one rule: *There are no rules.* The death and destruction that result from real air combat is much more lasting and real than anything depicted in the *Top Gun* movie or any other Hollywood film, and much more vicious than any marketplace face-off between business competitors.

Still, competing successfully in today's global business arena bears some interesting similarities to air combat—a remarkably fascinating, almost intoxicating, experience, in which those who compete are simultaneously the hunter and the hunted. The battleground of your marketplace can be demanding, exhilarating, and heart-stopping. Like the Aces, to achieve peak performance in your workplace "dogfights," you must bring your A-game every day. No excuses for being tired, distracted, overworked, or unprepared. As I learned in that heated battle over the steaming jungles of North Vietnam, if you want to win, you cannot blink under the unrelenting pressure of a well-trained enemy intent on shooting you down.

While you may never share the experience of taking a fighter jet into airborne combat, you are about to learn how to use the secrets of the flying Aces to win every time, to remain calm when things around you seem out of control, to guide yourself, your team, and your organization through even the toughest challenges against the most skillful and well-coordinated attacks. So let's get started; your training begins now.

Chapter One

THE ACES' PEAK PERFORMANCE FORMULA

*"The will to win is of little value
without the will to prepare."*
—Unknown

Is your workplace bombarding you relentlessly with unexpected problems and challenges from all directions? With all the recent budget cuts, downsizing, and rightsizing of personnel, has every day become another round of do-more-with-less? Is senior management's sole input to the organization something along the lines of "Get the job done now, no matter what"? And do you see conditions in your workplace improving, or are they mired in a downhill slide? If your answers to these questions leave you feeling beaten down by the pressure to boost your organizational and professional performance, you aren't alone.

Newer technologies were supposed to relieve some of the workplace pressures we all feel, but that hasn't happened. If anything, today's wired workplace has given us a nonstop avalanche of additional information to sort through as we struggle to meet more and tighter deadlines. There's rarely any downtime for planning long-term goals or assessing how well we're doing at managing operations and hitting milestones. As a result, we're caught in a continuous scramble to keep moving toward ever-shifting goals and to keep fighting a no-win game of catch-up with never-ending pressures from tough competitors, ever-changing technologies, new or revised company procedures, and new product lines.

Given the high-pressure stakes of business today, we shouldn't be surprised that decision makers at every level are feeling the heat of on-the-job stress. In a recent study by Northwestern Life Insurance Company, almost 50 percent of executives surveyed described their jobs as "very stressful." The *Harvard Business Review* notes that dealing with increasingly higher levels of workplace pressures—the leading cause of on-the-job stress—has become a top priority for senior management. I have heard this concern echoed in my own interviews with more than 200 executives from companies across the United States. Here's a sampling of the most common pressure points they reported:

- Mounting pressures from tight deadlines
- Ever-increasing stress from multiple projects
- Fiercely competitive workplace environment
- Understaffed departments
- Overworked/exhausted employees
- Tight or reduced budgets leading to increased demands to do more with less

In other words, organizations everywhere are being challenged to maximize their performance under sometimes overwhelming pressure. To best understand how to accomplish that goal, I suggest that we turn to a special group—Ace fighter pilots—to learn some invaluable lessons about making critical, game-changing decisions under the white heat of life-or-death pressure.

As you learned from the story of my own aerial combat experiences, dogfights are wildly unpredictable events that take fighter pilots through a fast-moving series of emotional–psychological peaks and valleys. The Aces who took part in those battles had to remain calm and effective while making constant life-or-death decisions under extreme pressure.

To give you an idea of what that daily pressure of flying air combat can do to a person, take a look at these pictures.

Source: Knight of Germany: Oswald Boelcke German Ace
by Professor Johannes Werner, published by Greenhill Books.

The picture on the left is of a young German fighter pilot named Oswald Boelcke, aged twenty-four; the picture on the right is that same Oswald Boelcke six months later, when he was the world's leading Ace with forty shoot-downs. Oswald Boelcke was not a hard-living man. He didn't drink, smoke, or carouse. He was a dedicated fighter pilot. So what happened to him? The same thing that could happen to any of us if we are not careful. The tension, stress, and unrelenting pressure for optimum workplace performance, if left unchecked, can take an awful toll. Certainly the consequences Boelcke faced if he failed were more severe than any workplace challenges. But we can learn a lot about the price of pressure from the lessons written on Oswald Boelcke's face.

The Aces' lives and those of their teammates depended on their ability to consistently produce strong performance, in every air combat mission, no matter what. The TOPGUN air combat training program was created for the purpose of preparing Navy flyers to do just that. The principles and practices that form the foundation for that training also make up the framework for the leadership approach you are about to learn—a six-part formula for maintaining peak performance in any high-pressure environment.

In this chapter, we're going to look at the Ace fighter pilot's approach to maintaining peak performance and how the same basic principles can help boost the performance of decision makers in the fast-moving, high-pressure atmosphere of most businesses today. Next, we will examine each of the elements included in the Peak Performance Formula so you can better understand how the ideas and practices they represent relate directly to your own ability to make winning decisions and to act quickly and decisively in any high-pressure situation. And because each of us must confront our own set of issues in the daily dogfight of business, the end of this chapter offers a short series of questions that can help you identify the issues that represent your greatest peak performance challenges.

Following the Formula, Step by Step

I'm often asked about the "secrets" to the successes of the fighter pilots who have gone on to become Aces. As I said earlier, the foundations of that training lie in principles, not secrets. Operating at peak performance under pressure is more than a catchy phrase—it's a specific process required for business success. Based on my own observations and those of the other Aces I've studied and interviewed, these three basic principles form the foundation of the Aces' approach to maintaining peak performance under intense pressure:

1. **Plan carefully and prepare relentlessly.** Aces spent a huge amount of time, much of it after-hours, getting ready for the next training flight and, later, the next combat mission. Not surprisingly, they achieved excellent results—which were the results they expected. None believed they would encounter a situation in combat they hadn't experienced in training. There's a saying that sums up the unshakable faith that these pilots hold in the role of relentless planning and preparation

for winning in air combat: *You will fight the way you train.* Those who think their gut instinct will help them rise to the occasion when the chips are down in combat or at work are in for a big surprise. Numerous studies on human behavior report that when the tension, anxiety, and stress are the greatest, whatever your line of work, you fall back on your level of training. Therefore, the Aces trained hard and trained realistically.

2. **Never let your focus waver.** As a group, the Aces were highly focused on *being* highly focused. They knew that the many, sometimes unpredictable, events of a combat mission could easily distract them unless they made attention to detail one of their primary goals. This intense focus complemented their burning desire to be the best at what they did, to push them to respond rapidly and correctly in even the most chaotic and life-threatening situations.

3. **Never stop working to get better.** The Aces were constantly driven by an unyielding aspiration to become better fighter pilots. They also were highly self-disciplined—a cornerstone habit they brought every day to all aspects of their performance. Together, these qualities enabled the Aces to remain committed to following the lessons and principles they learned in their training to continually improve their performance. They followed a simple mantra: *The day you stop wanting to get better is the day you stop being good.*

These guiding principles supported the Aces in the long, hard work of learning how to achieve brilliant combat results under incredibly stressful conditions. Now let's talk about you. Wouldn't you like to have some of that Ace fighter pilot ice-water in the veins when things get crazy at work? Who wouldn't want to remain calm and competent in the middle of a major workplace crisis? To help business leaders and decision makers like you leverage the same principles that helped the Aces win in any situation, and remain ultimately cool in the process, I have distilled those principles of the Aces into a six-part formula for achieving peak performance under pressure. Here are its elements:

1. **Planning**—The Aces built their wins on simple plans with measureable goals.

2. **Preparation**—Through relentless preparation, the Aces were always ready for any emerging threat or new development.

3. **Focus**—Unblinking focus and attention to detail enabled the Aces to act decisively in any situation.

4. **Assessment**—The Aces carefully and constantly measured their performance to find every possible means of making it better.

5. **Improvement**—The Aces were *never* satisfied with their performance, and they worked for continuous improvement.

6. **Self-Discipline**—The Aces' unwavering self-discipline enabled them to remain committed to following the lessons of their training and experience—all the time, every time.

Together, these elements create a powerful formula that enabled the Aces to consistently make the best decisions under the greatest emotionally challenging pressures imaginable.

$$\text{PLANNING + PREPARATION + FOCUS + ASSESSMENT + IMPROVEMENT + SELF-DISCIPLINE} = \text{PEAK PERFORMANCE}$$

By following this simple but powerful formula, you too can make good decisions and lead more effectively, even when faced with your toughest workplace challenges. Now let's take a closer look at each of these elements to see how they can work together to build your highest levels of performance.

Planning for Success

Today's jet fighter cockpit is a highly sophisticated, technological marvel providing pilots with an avalanche of information. Cockpits have more than 300 different switch positions, nine computers, eighty displays, and forty different audio tones. That's sensory overload!

In this complex and sometimes chaotic environment, the rapidly changing dynamics of air combat against an aggressive adversary, hell-bent on shooting you down, make every decision and maneuver critically important. Aces have always been acutely aware: success in air combat requires that they set basic, measurable goals and use simple, flexible plans. That's why planning is the first element in the Aces' formula.

Photo courtesy of C.J. "Heater" Heatley III.

Many executives today are working on complex, multifaceted projects requiring substantial resources and personnel from different departments, often at varying sites. The potential for profit is large. But so are the commitments of your time, sweat, and company resources. And senior management has left no doubt: *Get it done now, no excuses.*

So where do you begin? What should you do first? What resources do you need? Who and what can help you get things done more quickly? To answer these and the other endless questions that bombard the leaders of any project or organization, you can begin by following the Aces' proven practice of creating and following simple plans with measurable goals. While the Aces used this approach to plan for combat missions, you can apply it just as effectively to create winning daily, project, and even business plans.

When you simplify your goals and plans, you have a clear, actionable road map for achievement. You also are better prepared to tackle the most important things first and then keep going with well-defined priorities. Your carefully crafted plans provide you with a critical tool for making sure that every member of your team fully understands the goals you are pursuing and the tactics you plan to use in that effort. Educational psychologists tell us that the better your teammates understand what you're trying to achieve, the greater your chance of achieving it. The measurable goals attached to your plans enable you and your team to carefully track your progress and continually improve your performance along the way.

So how about your own approach to planning? Do you follow the Aces' approach to make sure your plans are simple and your business tactics are easy to perform? Is the structure of your meetings, presentations, and deals straightforward? Or do you sometimes use a structure that is incomplete, vague, disorganized, or too complicated for your people to understand? Do you struggle to stay current with emerging technologies, favoring hard-to-implement upgrades that you haven't fully mastered? Or maybe you think you're too busy or too experienced to even need a structured approach in your meetings, presentations, and deals. As you learn later in this book, your dedication to crafting simple, useful plans with clearly measurable goals will play a central role in your overall ability to achieve peak performance.

Preparing for Anything

While the principles and practices of careful planning are essential to every fighter pilot's training, Aces never forgot that planning alone won't guarantee success. *The most valuable thing you can bring into combat is a good, carefully thought-out plan,* the time-tested military axiom tells us. But it then goes on to say, *Many times, the first casualty of combat is your good, carefully thought-out plan.* So what do you do then?

The Aces' combat flying was, for the most part, reaction flying. In the heat of battle, there was no time to analyze alternatives. That's where relentless preparation, the second element of the Peak Performance Formula, comes into play. By thoroughly preparing for every combat mission—creating accurate mission plans based on the latest intelligence, reviewing tactical plans, checking and rechecking equipment, endlessly reviewing training and the lessons learned in recent missions—the Aces developed the knowledge and confidence necessary to respond to any event, as it happened, whether or not it was included in their plans. They knew that if they were surprised in combat, they were in trouble. And the same applies to you in today's volatile workplace, loaded with uncertainty, financial risk, and constant reordering of corporate priorities. Preparation is a potent tool for avoiding the added tension, anxiety, and stress of constant work-related surprises.

In the heat of your workday, you may have too little time to stop and weigh your options. Whether you're giving a major presentation, walking into a crucial client meeting, or finalizing an important contract, you can almost count on having to field unexpected curveballs and deal-killers. Even the most carefully constructed plans can be knocked sideways before 9:00 a.m. by a series of unplanned glitches.

Imagine this: When you first get to work, the company email isn't accessible because the server is down, the IT Help Desk has been called several times but has not responded, your assistant just informed you that your 11:00 conference call with a promising prospect has been moved up to 9:00, you can't locate that prospect's file, your cell phone battery is almost dead, you have two client calls on hold at your desk phone, one of your project managers needs a closed-door session with you ASAP to discuss a thorny personnel issue, and you're coming down with a nasty cold. You're already stressed out, and your day is barely under way.

Don't worry. The Ace practice of *relentless preparation* can help you recover from these rocky starts and still have a productive day. Instead of getting flustered, frustrated, and stressed out from unexpected events, your thorough preparation—knowing your mission, your business, and your strengths, risks, and capabilities, as well as your team's—will enable you to handle unforeseen developments, show your mettle, and continue moving ahead.

At the completion of their combat preparations, Aces always asked the final question: *At what point in this mission are we most vulnerable?* To help answer this question, fighter pilots put a premium on the what-if approach. They knew that if they had mentally rehearsed all of the most likely events and outcomes, or what-ifs, then when something unexpected happened—and it always did—they were mentally ready to respond. Their decisions were quick, instinctive, decisive, and correct. As you will learn in chapter 3, "Preparing to Win," I recommend that you take a few moments before every important presentation or client interaction to review the benefits your work brings to that group, to be intimately familiar with the facts and details, and anticipate objections, then think through your best responses with your team. That what-if exercise enables you to take every opportunity to emphasize the upside of your company's products, services, or ideas. Is this tooting your own horn? No—it is effective selling. Despite more than thirty years in business, I still write down a brief outline of the major points to cover in advance of tricky daily calls and meetings, and I keep this checklist with me during those events.

If you say that's a nice idea but you're too busy, *time out!* The meeting or phone call you spent several weeks setting up, the one that is pivotal to moving a big project ahead, is about to occur, but you're too busy to give yourself and your teammates a major-points outline? I suggest that you reconsider. Your competition is darn good. You'll need to be better if you're serious about winning the competitive battles of the workplace.

PREPARE TO TAKE THE LONG VIEW

Relentless preparation can help you see beyond the bumps that line your workday and focus on the goals you're working toward. Think about your daily meetings, phone calls, emails, and other communications. Some contain blunt, rude, incomplete, and false information. When you receive them, you can feel your gut start churning with increased stress, frustration, and anxiety. Now you're angry.

Your first impulse may be to send a blunt, even ruder response or an edgy reply that proves you're right and the other person is wrong. Instead, take the long view. Remember that all business relationships—with subordinates, senior management, clients, prospects, and vendors—can be fragile. Once strained, they are almost impossible to repair.

During tense work situations requiring your utmost tact and finesse, take some time to think through your best response. Before taking action, do a what-if analysis to review your options. Put yourself in a position to make your best decisions, without emotion. That kind of preparation is key to survival, in any high-pressure situation.

Maintaining Laser-Beam Focus

As you've just seen, the Aces remained committed to following simple plans and relentlessly preparing for their missions, so they could respond to the inevitable what-ifs that always arise in air combat. Anticipating the tough and chaotic conditions of combat, they trained themselves to pay attention to the most important details and to stay focused on the right things at the right times during their missions.

Focus is the third element in the Peak Performance Formula, and a major point of emphasis in TOPGUN's curriculum. TOPGUN instructors demand that the students treat every training flight like it were a combat sortie requiring them to pay close attention to what they should do at critical airborne times, avoid distractions, and limit multitasking. Instructors want students to fully understand that the most important maneuver of their entire flight career is the one they are about to do next. Students must learn to block out everything else, so they can focus exclusively on the task at hand.

Keep in mind that the closer you get to presentation day, deal closing, or project completion, the more details you need to manage and the greater the pressure is on you to perform. As we've seen, pressures come from many sources, including unforeseen problems, last-minute obstacles, unexpected delays, personnel issues, and schedule conflicts. The better able you are to remain aware and on top of the details associated with your tasks, the more effectively you will be able to deal with these pressures. If your focus wavers, these pressures can suddenly mushroom. Then they can get you wired tighter with tension, anxiety, and stress—not the feelings you want dominating you and your workdays as critical deadlines approach.

As you will learn in chapter 4, "Maintaining Focus," TOPGUN instructors use a careful review, called a *mission debrief,* to help students improve their ability to grasp the details of what is actually taking place in their training dogfights, rather than relying on what they *think* is happening—a skill TOPGUN calls situational awareness (SA). Then we help them use that information to learn how to adjust their focus correctly to fit the circumstances. The rule is simple: good SA leads to good focus, which is essential for strong performance. And how do you develop good SA? By learning to block out all but the most essential elements of the task at hand, pay attention to what you're doing, and avoid all distractions.

For organizational leaders and decision makers, the link between focus and performance is equally strong. The better your ability to hone your focus and pay attention to the critical details of your operation, the better your results—and those of your team—will be. As you learn later in this book, the techniques for developing a laser-beam focus are quite simple. If you spend much of your workday bouncing from one crisis to another, for example, you can use the steps outlined in chapter 4 to get back on track: take a close look at the relevant events surrounding your most important issues, pick out the two or three top items, do a detailed analysis of the successes and missteps you're experiencing in your work with those items, and then follow a well-planned process to get them back on track to achieve your goals. You also will learn specific techniques for identifying the 25 percent of clients or projects that are most critical to your bottom line and for developing the skill of listening like a leader. Then you can always be attuned to the ideas, issues, and events that will play the most important role in achieving your goals. With this kind of unwavering focus, you can better see the road ahead.

Measuring Results Against Expectations

What's an effective way to measure your performance on the job? How do you know your decisions and actions are working as planned? Once more, let us follow the lead of the Aces as we consider the fourth element of their Peak Performance Formula—ongoing assessment.

As I mentioned earlier, at TOPGUN, we use debriefing to help students assess their performance in all training flights. Debriefs are systematic assessments designed to obtain useful performance-evaluation feedback by asking the students to compare their briefed plans with their airborne results. This assessment is also where the students get their lessons learned, through takeaways such as:

- What worked today, and why did it work?
- What didn't work today, and why didn't it?
- What corrective actions could improve my outcomes?

As you will learn in chapter 5, you can ask the same types of questions of yourself, your team, even your clients, to assess the strengths and weaknesses of your performance. If you are in sales, for example, how many new prospects did you contact this week? How many deals did you close? How many did you start or move forward? Are you meeting production and customer delivery schedules? In team debriefs, you might ask similar questions: Is the team on target to achieve its weekly, monthly, quarterly, and annual performance goals? If not, then why not, and how far off target are you? What has been working? Not working? Why? What changes are needed, and in what areas, for immediate improvement?

Do you see yourself as a top-performer-in-training? I hope your answer is a resounding *Yes!* That was the Aces' answer. That's why the Aces viewed their assessments as essential preparation for combat. Look at your assessments in the same light. Sure, these "debriefings" may sound like boring, even unproductive, parts of your day. They can be just that, if you're uninterested in growing your skills. But without some type of regularly scheduled team performance assessment, you will most likely continue plodding along, repeating the same mistakes. Ongoing assessments are fundamental tools for performing at your best when nothing short of your best will be required of you. Make them a habit for you and your team.

Improving Continuously

The bitter disappointment that comes from failing to do something when you had every chance to do it is best summarized by the poet John Greenleaf Whittier: "The saddest words of tongue or pen: the words *it might have been*." Planning, preparation, focus, and assessment are all key practices for decision makers who never want to utter those fateful words, but none of these elements of the Peak Performance Formula is more essential for maximizing your performance than the fifth one: nonstop improvement. This element has a simple premise—the Aces' mantra you will see woven throughout this book: *The day you stop wanting to be better is the day you stop being good.*

Aces centered all of their training around becoming the very best fighter pilots in the world. Steady improvement was something they expected every day and pursued with vigor. That is how they became Aces. Any consistently successful athlete, sports team, or business leader understands that constant improvement is paramount for sustained success. My interviews with Aces indicated they were obsessed with doing whatever it took to get better. They had a burn-ing desire, from early in their careers, to do what was necessary to become the very best they could be. In fact, they all were hell-bent on being absolutely the best fighter pilots in the history of military aviation. They expected to dominate their competition, whether in training or combat, and they did.

Over my military career, I have noted that one of the main dif-ferences between Aces and other fighter pilots is that many of those "others," often those who needed training the most, were satisfied with their performance and seldom improved. Make no mistake, most fighter pilots are very good aviators. But those who never achieved peak performance had no personal or team-improvement program in place. They didn't think one was necessary. On the other hand, of the more than 400 fighter pilots I have flown with and against, the 3 percent who were superstars were *never* satisfied with their performance. They always worked to improve, 24/7, and never let up. There's no such thing as a natural combat fighter pilot. Those who became Aces were committed to one of the most basic ingre-dients for combat success: hard work. Like the Aces, your future success isn't based on a right-of-passage or an entitlement over time. Rather, it's the product of your hard work.

I have always had the greatest respect for highly motivated busi-ness executives with a strong work ethic, doing what it takes every day to get better. By raising their own performance bar, they often help boost the performance of everyone around them. As author Jim Collins notes in his bestselling book, *Good to Great: Why Some Companies Make the Leap . . . and Others Don't*, without a commit-ment to constant improvement, it's almost impossible to realize your full potential. People who are self-satisfied or content to wing it can be disastrously unprepared to lead effectively under pressure. On their best days, they will remain just average. Who wants to trust that kind of leadership in today's economy?

Continuous performance improvement requires commitment, but it remains a relatively straightforward process. In chapter 6,

"Maximizing Performance," you will learn a number of techniques and routine practices for building individual and team performance, from developing unshakable confidence to honing your ability to interact with and influence others to developing key leadership skills and maximizing your credibility with clients and prospects. And as you'll learn, improving your skills sets up a circular pattern of successes and achievements that contribute to even better performance going forward.

Committing to Peak Performance

All of the preceding elements of the Peak Performance Formula are critical to the training and preparation of every Ace fighter pilot. All of them require *and* contribute to the sixth and final element of that formula—unwavering *self-discipline*. This element can be summed up with one simple direction: *Follow every element of the Peak Performance Formula, every day.*

That is what the Aces did as a matter of course throughout their flying careers. They knew that combat success wasn't about flying well on occasion—it was about being ready to fly to the best of their ability every day, regardless of the situation. Peak performance was their burning goal every day in training, and pursuing that goal paid them huge dividends in combat. They became Aces because they took no shortcuts in their preparations. That's why they relied on the elements of planning, preparation, focus, assessment, and improvement every day in training. They persevered and were fanatically dedicated in their quest to be the very best. When they got into combat and the heat was on, they were ready. They never deviated. They exercised tremendous self-discipline. That's how they became Ace fighter pilots.

Many other fighter pilots were on the same missions as the Aces and had the same opportunities, but more than 90 percent of them never shot down even one enemy airplane. Ever notice that some in your workplace are satisfied to achieve average (at best) results day after day? But a few—the aces of your organization or industry—knock it out of the park every day. They are doing what all the others in your profession have the same opportunities to do but don't. And self-discipline is the beating heart of their success.

The Aces relied on battle-tested lessons of air combat—what had worked for others and for them. They knew that their initial flying success could prompt deviation from the formula that produced it. Formula adjustments are a good idea and can work well. Formula deviations are usually a bad idea and can cause a whole new set of problems. What do you do when one of your projects at work or client relationships is initially successful? Do you take this success for granted? Do you think you have all the answers? Do you think that your client will remain loyal? Do you deviate from the techniques that brought success? Do you take your eye off the ball, drop your focus and let up? Do you start taking shortcuts? These can be dangerous decisions and have potentially disastrous results.

Remember that shifting from the basics of your business plan for no good reason is a risky strategy, even in the best of times. In chapter 7, "Maintaining Excellence Through Self-Discipline," you will learn how to use the skills you have gained throughout the book to avoid the most common—and damaging—workplace ambushes. You also learn how rigorously following the Peak Performance Formula and the principles it represents can help you defend the core values on which you have built your performance standards and eliminate self-inflicted setbacks that can undercut your progress. As in any powerful formula, the individual elements of planning, preparation, focus, assessment, and ongoing improvement are important all on their own, but they don't achieve their full potential until they are combined. Employing all of these elements, every day, requires real commitment and determination to be the best, all the time, every time. That's why unwavering self-discipline is the final, essential element in the Peak Performance Formula.

Chapter Debrief

Each year I speak at approximately forty corporate conventions and training events. I don't give canned presentations. By taking advantage of modern technology, I have access to extensive research and background information on my audiences. I start with the company's website, then Google it. Business sites such as www.hoovers.com also provide excellent additional information. After my research, I interview two or three of the most senior company executives over the phone. Each thirty-minute interview is one-on-one with the selected executive.

My purpose is to pinpoint the biggest sources of workplace strengths, weaknesses, pressures, challenges, accomplishments, and failures affecting their people (who will be the audience in my upcoming presentation) from the senior executives' perspective. I'm also interested in learning what leadership strategies these executives use to address their challenges, and how well those strategies are working to help their teams achieve peak performance. This Q&A exercise enables me to identify the most critical peak performance challenges these individuals and organizations are facing, as well as the types of solutions they have used to work on these challenges and their relative successes or failures. From interviewing these senior executives over the past seventeen years, I have found that all business types in all geographic quadrants of our country are struggling with similar types of issues.

Here, I've listed the questions I typically ask of my clients, along with their most common responses. I've also listed a few tactical questions similar to those we at TOPGUN might ask in our student debriefs to help you further consider the issues raised by their responses. Finally, I've left some spaces at the end of each of these question groups where you can fill in your own thoughts and responses. Better yet, pick a point or two that match your current problems at work. Discuss them at your next team meeting with a keen ear tuned to what your teammates think are the best solutions.

Q } What do you consider to be the three primary
strengths of your people? What do they do well?

   1. "They understand our core business. They know our
product lines and how we fit in our industry."

- What about you and your people? Do you/
they have a strong nuts-and-bolts grasp of your
business/industry?

- Are you/they trained properly? Is your training
program current and ongoing? What can you do
to improve your company's training?

- Are you using the latest technology to most
effectively run your business? Or do you play
technology catch-up?

   2. "Our people have great 'numbers awareness.' They
understand what it takes for us to be profitable."

- Can you make the same claim? How does your
actual revenue compare with projected annual,
quarterly, and monthly revenue?

- Is your profitability matrix valid today? When did
you last update or modify it?

   3. "Our people handle adversity well."

- How do you deal with adversity and problems at
work?

- Are your problem-solving methods effective?

- How do you know? How do you measure them?

Your response: _____

_____

_____

_____

Q } What four areas of your or your team's overall
performance need improvement?

   1. "Accountability. We all talk about it, but we don't do
much about it."

- What about you—how's your accountability index?

- What needs to change to improve your accountability? When?

- How do you plan to measure accountability for yourself and your team?

- Can you sustain a meaningful accountability policy? How?

2. "Delegation. With so much work on my desk, and so little time, I need to get better at delegating."

   - How good are you at delegating? Are you receptive to it? Why, or why not?

   - How will you monitor your delegation efforts?

   - How will you know if you are delegating effectively?

3. "Follow-up. We talk about it constantly, but based on what I hear from our customers, we're still not very good at it."

   - How's *your* follow-up? Are you satisfied with it? Are others satisfied with your follow-up?

   - What needs to change to get better at follow-up? When?

   - How do you measure follow-up?

   - How do you plan to communicate the results of your efforts to improve follow-up with your people?

4. "Problem identification. We need to identify problem areas sooner so we can take corrective action quicker."

   - How are your inter-department and intra-company communications working? Can they get better? How?

   - What about your daily operations—are they characterized by a *proactive* or *reactive* management style?

   - Do you go from crisis to crisis every day?

   - What corrections can you make to reduce crises and reactive-management situations?

Your response: _____

_____

_____

_____

Q}
When you look out at your business horizon over the next twelve to eighteen months, what are the three top challenges you see bearing down on you?

1. "We need to increase revenues *today.*"

   - Do you have a plan for increasing revenues?

   - What specifically can you or senior management do to best help you plan?

   - What are the elements of your plan? What do you intend to do differently? When do you plan to start?

   - How will you measure the effectiveness of your plan?

2. "We all need to better manage our changing business."

   - What are you doing to address the changes in your business/industry?

   - Who besides you is identifying and analyzing these changes?

   - How are you prioritizing your items for change?

   - What actions do you plan? When?

   - What method will you use to measure the effectiveness of your changes? When and how will you know if you are making the right changes?

3. "We need to create more customer value for our products and services than our competitors are offering."

   - Where do you rate your customer value proposition compared with your competition?

   - What are your competitors doing now better than you?

   - What are you doing now better than your competitors?

- How can you negate or reduce your competitors' strengths with your customers?
- How can you enhance your customer relationships against growing competition?

Your response: _____

_____

_____

_____

Q } If you could wave a magic wand now and implement one change that would have the most immediate positive impact on your productivity, what would you change?

1. "We'd like to have a sustainable strategic plan in place."

    - Is your current strategic plan sustainable? Why, or why not?
    - When was the last time you reviewed your strategic plan?
    - What do you need to adjust or modify to make it more sustainable in today's economy?

2. "We need to better anticipate challenges and to make better decisions."

    - Are you ever able to see workday challenges and problems before they occur? Why, or why not?
    - Do daily challenges and problems regularly blindside you? What causes these blindsides?
    - What corrective action have you taken to reduce your blindsides?

3. "Everyone needs to pitch in to help us identify new product/service opportunities."

    - How do you currently identify new product/service opportunities?
    - What is the success rate of your current method?
    - What new products or services have you introduced in the past twelve months?

- What new products or services do you plan to introduce in the next twelve months?

- How does this translate into increased profits? What's your "increased profits" target?

4. "We must continually refocus company assets on the right projects."

   - Do your most important projects have the right personnel and resources working on them? Why, or why not? What percentage of the time would you say that personnel and assets are deployed on the wrong projects?

   - When will you or your organization refocus personnel and assets?

   - Is your method of refocusing personnel and assets sustainable? For how long? Then what?

   - How do you plan to measure results?

Your response: _____

_____

_____

_____

Q} When thinking about their jobs, what is it that you think keeps your people awake at night?

1. "Will they have a job tomorrow?"

2. "Can they handle the constant pressures at work?"

3. "Will they find the time to get everything done?"

4. "Will we ever change our reactive management?"

5. "When will they be given consistent, clear direction and expectations?"

Your response: _____

_____

_____

_____

Q } When thinking about your job, what is it that keeps you awake at night?

1. "I worry about our business failing."

2. "Can we remain a viable business in today's global economy?"

3. "Is one of our competitors about to introduce a newer, better product, at a cheaper price, to our customers?"

4. "Are we hiring the right people? Are we assigning them to the right jobs?"

5. "Can we retain the right people?"

Your response: _____

_____

_____

_____

Q } When your people leave our presentation, what one thing do you want foremost in their mind?

1. "We want them more excited about their work."

2. "We're looking for a boost in employee hope."

3. "We'd like to see them better equipped to deal with high-pressure situations."

4. "I'd like them to understand the importance of more focused leadership."

5. "We all need to communicate more effectively."

6. "They need to understand the importance of executing better than our competition."

Now for your response: What's the most important takeaway you hope to gain from this book? _____

_____

_____

_____

As I mentioned in the introduction, every chapter in this book will end with a short debriefing to help you think about the ideas offered in the chapter and how you might use those ideas to improve upon your current methods and approaches to addressing related workplace challenges. I hope the short Q&A exercise in this chapter debrief has helped you identify the most critical overall challenges you and your organization are experiencing. By thinking about these issues, questions, and answers, you can be better prepared to use the ideas and techniques you will read about in the chapters ahead to address the specific obstacles that might be keeping you and your organization from achieving peak performance—each time, every time, no matter how much workplace tension, anxiety, and pressure surround you. Just like the Aces.

CHAPTER TWO

PLANNING TO WIN

"A goal without a plan is just like a wish."
—ANTOINE DE SAINT-EXUPÉRY

The world's all-time leading Ace, the Ace of Aces, is Erich Hartmann of the German Luftwaffe. During World War II, he was credited with shooting down 352 planes. He flew more than 1,400 combat missions over thirty months. During his last twelve months of combat flying, Hartmann flew four or five missions every day, piloting one of four German fighter planes against more than 100 allied planes. In all his missions, against overwhelming odds, he never had a wingman shot down. Hartmann himself, however, was shot down seventeen times—and on two different occasions, he was shot down *twice* in the same day.

In a mid-1990s interview, I asked Hartmann how he had dealt with the incredible daily strain of flying combat. He said simply, "I knew every flight was going to be tough. I expected it. But I never looked back except to learn from my mistakes. At night, I had my meal, my drink, and my rest. In the morning, I was fit again and ready to go." This simple plan enabled Hartmann to handle extreme pressure and to excel in the incredibly dangerous environment of air combat.

Planning—creating simple plans with measurable goals—is the first element in the Peak Performance Formula for good reason. In a combat dogfight, many factors beyond the Aces' control were in play and situations could change in an instant. The Aces knew that the quality of their decisions under fire would determine their chances for success, so they reviewed all combat plans thoroughly with their team before implementation. Many times, they would adjust their original plans, based on their teammates' input or the latest intelligence data. As a result of this careful planning, the Aces went into combat with a full range of potential actions and outcomes and the latest intelligence fresh in their minds. They were confident that when the pressure of combat dogfights spiked up, their planning had prepared them to make the decisions necessary to win.

In today's fast-moving, unpredictable business world, decision makers need to be able to rely on a solid what-if planning process too. To be an effective decision maker, you cannot afford to appear unprepared, timid, confused, or lacking in confidence. To put it bluntly, nobody is fooled by a bullshitter—the ill-prepared, disorganized executive who is winging it, making weak decisions or none at all. The decisions you make today on the fly will determine if, and to what degree, you succeed tomorrow. Without a solid, workable plan, with clearly designated milestones, you can't make the kinds of decisions necessary to keep moving forward in the face of the many unexpected roadblocks and potholes that litter your workday.

Well-crafted plans enable decision makers to act confidently and decisively in the face of even the most unexpected developments and greatest competitive pressures. Clearly designated, measurable goals in your plans offer key milestones for determining that your progress is on time and on track. That way, everyone on your team knows precisely where they are, where they're headed, and how they're going to get there. Keep in mind that old business axiom: *If it isn't measured, it can't be managed.*

You may agree that this first element in the Aces' formula has significant value—if only you could find the time to incorporate it into your daily routine. I find, however, that many of us already invest time in creating plans but then fail when it comes to implementation. As you learn in this chapter, the time you invest in planning can pay huge dividends. Planning before big meetings, conference calls, and client interactions boosts both your confidence and your effectiveness. Clients, prospects, teammates, colleagues, and senior management notice how you handle these interactions and will remember your performance when making their own decisions about whether they want to work with you.

What are your targeted goals for today, tomorrow, next week, next month, next quarter, and next year? The ideas you learn here will give you the tools you need to identify and achieve those goals, by creating and following a workable plan. This chapter outlines the three types of planning essential to any business and any career—*strategic, operational,* and *tactical* planning—and their roles in a well-crafted business plan. We also will walk through the four no-fail steps for creating a daily action plan that enables you to accomplish the tasks you *must* attend to, every day, in an effective and timely manner. As you are about to learn, no matter what type of planning you are engaged in, your plans will be more effective, and your performance more powerful, when you follow the blueprint for simplicity and accountability laid out in this element of the Aces' formula.

Acing the Three Types of Business Planning

Most of the people I address in my speaking engagements and business consultations tell me they have a written business plan. Writing a business plan is a critical first step in setting out the goals, strategies, and tactics of the organization. But an equally important next step in that process is following and regularly reviewing the plan. That's where many decision makers stumble.

We all know that the business cycle is always either expanding or contracting. When it expands, new prospects emerge, deals get closed, revenue increases, and executives look good. When the cycle contracts, clients cut back and deals take longer to complete—they might be put on hold or canceled altogether. Executives try to hold their ground as everything about their operation is scrutinized. In the down cycle, organizations make cuts and implement changes as unpredictable levels of uncertainty emerge.

Whatever the state of the cycle, you want to be clear about where you are on the curve and then make necessary adjustments to your business plans. Your goal is to know your plan well and to be ever vigilant so you can stay out in front of the business cycles. In today's highly competitive global economy, standing still is tantamount to falling behind. Sticking with outdated goals and plans is a dangerous strategy that could prove damaging to the company and fatal to your job and career if left unchecked. And you can't keep your business plan attuned to future growth if you don't know its current state.

When I ask my audiences for a show of hands indicating how many have reviewed their plan since it was written, about 20 percent raise their hands. Nearly all admit that they had only briefly glanced at their business plan once in the past year. Then I ask the audience how many have written out their own personal business plan for the year. Now maybe 10 percent raise their hands. That's a pretty casual approach to the whole process of business planning in comparison to the Aces, who painstakingly reviewed their combat plans every day.

TOPGUN takes the same approach, reviewing flight and training plans daily, weekly, monthly, quarterly, and annually. TOPGUN uses this process to ensure that students achieve planned training goals while performing up to the program's high standards. If planning reviews reveal that certain goals remain unmet or a particular student's performance isn't up to TOPGUN's standards, instructors adjust the plans to address corrective actions. If, after implementing the plan revisions, the student's performance fails to improve to TOPGUN criteria, the student is dropped from the course. Sound harsh? Then think about the fact that these instructors are putting the lives of their students and teammates on the line when training these aviators for combat.

VIEWING YOUR BUSINESS PLAN FROM THE ACES' PERSPECTIVE

Take a moment to consider the way you approach your organization's business plan in comparison to the way the Aces created and used their combat plans. Have you read your business plan recently? Why, or why not? Do you periodically review it? Do you even have one? Have you shared your business plan with your team? Did they offer input, and have you taken that input into consideration? Have you made or suggested updates to the plan to make it more effective? What one change could have the most immediate and positive impact on your daily performance? Considering these questions can help you become more engaged with the business plan that guides your work and determines your professional success and that of your organization's overall mission.

Now, think about your office and your workday. Your decisions put your job, your career, and the jobs and careers of your teammates and those whose jobs depend on you on the line. When anyone on your team fails to understand and meet key goals, the entire team and its performance will suffer. When your business plan no longer targets the right goals or fails to define effective strategic direction, the health of your organization and the professional "life" of everyone there is at risk.

In all business planning, decision makers must consider the three main planning categories—*strategic, operational,* and *tactical.* Let's take a closer look at each of these categories to understand their roles in building—and maintaining—a simple, effective business plan.

Taking the Long View: Strategic Planning

Strategic planning focuses on long-term goals. From the 1990s through 2006, long-term planning typically meant three to five years ahead. Then came the financial crisis, a major stock market downturn on Wall Street and around the globe, substantial job losses, massive federal bailouts of large corporations, new federal government regulations, and a restructuring of our financial institutions. The real possibility of other countries going bankrupt and the ongoing threat of global terrorism and conflict in the Middle East only added to the risk and uncertainty in the global economy. That's too many unforeseen events happening too fast with unknown consequences. In response, many companies trimmed their strategic outlook to no longer than eighteen months. Most decision makers today consider strategic plans that go beyond that to be obsolete.

What does strategic planning mean to you? As a business consultant, here's how I have advised senior executives to consider that question: if they could look out into the next eighteen months of their company's operation, what would they ideally like to see regarding:

- Gross income, expenses, net operating income, and market share
- The number of employees retained, hired, lost, or reassigned, and in what departments those changes took place
- The number of geographic operating locations, profit centers, and new product or service types
- The number of clients gained and lost, and the number of new prospects in the pipeline

These questions should have carefully researched, market-based answers for comparison with today's actual performance. As with my consulting clients, your answers to these questions form the foundation of your strategic plan. This is your vision for your company's future and the role you see for yourself in shaping that future. In formulating your responses, be bold. Senator Robert Kennedy once said about the future, "Some men see things as they are and ask why; I see things that never were and ask, why not?" When devising the goals for your strategic plan, ask yourself, Why not?

Make sure that important elements of your strategic plan are reflected in what you do every day at work. Otherwise, you will look at your career, your job, and your company's future through a badly out-of-focus lens. Sure you're busy every day, working to get things done. But are they the *right* things? And do you have any idea where you are headed? A well-crafted strategic plan provides an essential filter for your daily decisions and keeps you on track and advancing toward your long-term goals—making your workdays more productive, not just busy.

Planning for Resources: Operational Planning

Operational planning refers to the resources needed to deliver your goods and services on time and on budget to your customers or clients. As the business cycle changes, you're tasked with a continuing "needs assessment" analysis regarding resources. The TOPGUN instructors use these same types of ongoing analyses to be certain that their training facilities, support services, and equipment are the tools they need to train combat pilots to win against ever-evolving enemy threats. In my forty-three years in Naval Aviation, there have been twelve new versions of the Sidewinder heat-seeking missile used in combat, each more sophisticated and deadly than the last. Without TOPGUN's vigilant operational planning, today's fighter pilots wouldn't have the necessary training and resources to combat current and emerging threats.

If you want to survive in your industry, you have to deal with the same types of evolving resource needs. Do you have the right number of employees for the different skill sets your business requires? Are you the right size? Do you have adequate office, warehouse, and distribution space? Do you have the right technology and know-how to take advantage of what that space offers? What new technologies would you like to have? Why? At what cost? If your operational plan is more than a few years old, it may need dramatic revision, since today's answers to those questions will be much different from those of even a year ago. And next year's answers will be different as well.

That's why you want to regularly review and update the operational planning elements of your business plan. You want to make sure you have the right assets in place for the challenges ahead. And don't forget to link up any significant changes in operational planning to your strategic plan.

In these volatile times, it's tougher getting a firm grip on future resource needs. Consider personnel, for example. According to the U.S. Department of Labor, between 2007 and 2010, eight million people nationwide lost jobs and some four million more entered the U.S. labor market. That shift set up a buyer's market for employers that is still thriving as I write this book. Highly qualified people are looking for jobs that you may have available. But, at some point, that will change. As an employer, these shifts present you with many questions: when to hire, how many to hire, and in which jobs. Will you need new facilities? Or should your organization combine or downsize existing facilities? Should these facilities be located near your present location, in a different state, or overseas? Your operational plan will determine the best answers to these and many other resource acquisition and allocation questions.

Changing economic realities aren't the only shifts that require a new business model with revised assumptions. Thanks to technology, worker efficiency and productivity have increased significantly, and software has substantially reduced the number of people required to perform most jobs. Today, many companies are closing offices and reducing personnel, even as they ship more products and provide expanded services. Organizations still following old models and assumptions in their operational planning are set up for failure—they just don't know it (yet).

When the fog of economic uncertainty lifts—as it most surely will—and economic growth picks up, the strength of your organization's answers to these questions will determine whether it is well positioned for a quick "resource response." Decision makers without a current, carefully constructed operational plan ready for implementation may lose significant business to the competition. Conversely, those companies with a solid operational plan in place will be best positioned to increase their customer base and market share when the market improves.

As the Aces knew, being unaware of potential trouble can be a fatal mistake. Aviation history shows that approximately 80 percent of all pilots shot down in air combat had no idea they were in trouble until enemy bullets or missiles smashed into their planes. That's what happened to many of the pilots the Aces shot down. One minute, they were flying along straight and level over enemy airspace. Then in a split second, a barrage of bullets exploded in their cockpit and the plane erupted in flames.

Photo courtesy of C.J. "Heater" Heatley III.

As a decision maker, a catastrophe in your business won't cost you your life, but failing to plan for today's challenges *and* tomorrow's resource needs could cost you your job and your career. Even if you survive, you've exposed yourself and your organization to unnecessary risk. Creating a well-crafted operational plan is an important safeguard to protect against unexpected developments and competitive attacks.

Setting a Course for Daily Actions: Tactical Planning

Tactical planning organizes what you do every day—think of it as your organizational daily to-do list. Many of the decision makers I've interviewed have said they do a good job of creating and implementing tactical plans. Yet just as many admit they incorporate few strategic or operational planning concerns in their daily tactical routines. That can be a risky strategy.

So why does something as simple-sounding as a daily action plan require elements of strategic and operational planning? The answer to that is simple—and we've already discussed some of its implications in earlier sections of this chapter. Organizational leaders who fail to include strategic and operational planning elements in their daily action list may be slow to respond to changing economic, technological, or market conditions. When any of those conditions shift, as they most surely will, leaders without current strategic and operational elements in their business plan could be

BRINGING YOUR TEAM ON BOARD

To make your business plan truly effective, you also need to review its goals with your teammates, emphasizing each person's role in achieving those goals. Be specific. Even long-term plans need clear completion dates. Continually emphasize the obvious elements involved in achieving your goals, particularly with newer, younger team members. Many times, a failure to complete the obvious tasks causes the biggest problems—in combat and at work. The more members of your team who understand your goals, the greater will be your chances of achieving them. Getting input from your team (and senior management and mentors) is another way to make sure your plans are well crafted and have the full support of everyone involved faced with potentially disastrous results. This could translate into across-the-board losses in market share, clients, prospects, new opportunities, jobs, and revenue. If you get caught in any of these outcomes, rest assured that you will find yourself working under peak pressure. Without those strategic and operational inputs, however, the likelihood that you can achieve consistent peak performance is low. With strong daily plans that reflect larger strategic and operational planning and goals, you can avoid being washed off-course in the wake of change.

This relationship of strategic, operational, and tactical planning should be viewed as a living continuum. Your strategic plan is the foundation. It establishes *where* you are going and informs and influences all downstream decisions. The operational plan establishes how you are going to get there by identifying the tools you'll need. It also provides a road map for how you will execute your daily tactical plan. Over time, as regular reviews will highlight, changes in your

---

in their implementation. Educational psychologists tell us that plans are much more likely to be accepted by your staff if you first seek their input.

My experience from years of interviewing senior executives indicates that few of them discuss the strategic and operational elements of their plans with staff and teammates. Most agree that regular staff discussions are a good idea, but then they say they are too busy putting out fires or working on tricky projects with tight deadlines. They claim they don't have the time now but might consider these meetings later in the year. Some even contend that the company is doing fine and that the strategic and operational aspects of the business plan don't apply to their department.

Do you think these answers work in today's economy?

tactical landscape will prompt changes in your operational and strategic plans. This approach will help keep your plans linked as you execute your daily action plan. It will also help you keep current and responsive to change while engaging everyone on your team from top to bottom.

Getting the Most From a Daily Action Plan: Four No-Fail Steps

In preparing for those nerve-wracking, life-or-death dogfights, the Aces were always aware of the importance of getting the right things done at the right time, no matter what. All fighter pilots had the same opportunities to prepare the same way for combat. What set the Aces apart? The answer is that basically the Aces followed a plan for doing a series of seemingly little things that prepared them well for any eventuality. To the Aces, the seemingly small details of their daily activities added up to the big things that could make the difference between winning or losing. That same well-planned approach to taking care of the daily activities of business also separates an organization's ordinary decision makers from its superstars.

You know the importance of getting the right things done at the right time at work. Your future, the survival of your company, and your job all depend on it. But consider two questions about your approach to your daily activities: First, what are you doing right now to maximize your daily performance? Second, are you making every day count—or do you sometimes just go through the motions? At TOPGUN, instructors make sure that they and each of their students maximize daily performance by establishing and accomplishing ambitious daily goals. Here is the four-step process TOPGUN instructors use to create and implement those effective daily action plans:

1. Start every day by writing down a carefully thought-out plan.
2. Rank priorities within the plan.

3. Tackle activities according to priority.

4. Review progress at intervals throughout the day.

Let's take a closer look at each of these steps and how they can help you improve your daily workplace performance.

Step 1: Start Every Day by Writing Down a Carefully Thought-Out Plan

After arriving at work, what is the first thing you do? Many executives, myself included, go directly to their computers and check email, Twitter, LinkedIn, Facebook, and other accounts used for business purposes. (I have separate social media and email accounts for my personal communications, a practice I recommend for making the best use of your time at work.) In fact, many check their email and voice messages well before arriving at work to see what happened overnight that may require immediate action. With their electronic communications up to date, many senior decision makers then choose to cruise the floor and chat with the other early arrivals.

The younger teammates most likely remain glued to their electronic devices and use them as their vehicle of choice for communication. Perhaps if the seniors and juniors "cross-pollinated" their communications, your department might run more effectively. By cross-pollinating, I mean that the seniors become more adept at social media communications and the juniors become more skilled with personal, face-to-face communications. How can you do this? Set up your teams with a mix of senior and junior members. Listen to them, train them, and train yourself. Then communicate in the method that works best for your clients, prospects, senior management, subordinates, colleagues, and vendors. The age factor is a huge issue in deciding the best way to communicate. When I call my two kids, both in their mid-twenties, I might get a return call within a day if I'm lucky. But when I send them a text message, I usually get a response within five minutes. You see the point.

The first thing all TOPGUN instructors do after checking their electronic communications is to make a careful review of the plan-of-the-day (POD), distributed to all instructors late the previous afternoon. The POD is nothing more than a priority listing of that day's flights, ground-school lectures, and squadron training. It serves as the TOPGUN to-do list, setting the agenda, citing who does what and when. If an event is on the schedule at TOPGUN, department heads and instructors expect it to be completed in an outstanding manner.

Whether you end your day by drawing up tomorrow's daily action plan, or you create the plan when you come into work each morning, you too need to begin each day with a well-constructed plan that lists all of that day's essential activities. Numerous studies on effective workplace habits have concluded that a written plan increases your chances of completing necessary tasks by 90 percent.

As a leadership consultant, I always counsel my clients to

SCHEDULING PHONE TIME

A written daily action plan is a great source for determining your priority phone log—today's must-calls. Many time-management experts agree that this strategy of using your scheduled phone time to make and return the *right* calls from a preplanned list plays a crucial role in maximizing your daily performance.

Begin with a studied, written plan and a prioritized phone log. Schedule a specific time each day to make those calls. Used properly, your phone log can enhance your productivity. Whether you keep phone records on your phone, laptop, desktop, handheld device, notebook, or other device is less important than a structured recall system noting who said what to whom, what action items emerged, and the follow-up dates you set.

avoid the big mistake that I made early in my business career. Then, I believed I had a good feel for what needed to be done each day at work, so I didn't need to spend my valuable time writing out a daily action plan. I was too busy. Besides, as a TOPGUN instructor and a seasoned member of Naval Aviation's jet fighter community, I already had ample organizational experience. After struggling for several years in sales, however, I went back to my old TOPGUN organizational habits and began drawing up and following a daily action plan. The change in my performance was astounding. I won the Top Producer Award in my office four of the next six years, finished in the top five for fifteen consecutive years, and was rated the Top Office Leasing Specialist in my office for eighteen straight years.

I'm not talking about a lengthy or complex process for creating these daily action plans. Instead, I recommend that you follow the Aces' practice of creating simple plans with measurable goals. Keep your daily action plan brief and specific. Spend no more than fifteen minutes writing it. List every business and personal project you need to touch that day. Be specific and thorough and include clearly defined completion dates.

Next, review the projects to make sure they all belong on your plate. Which of them can you eliminate or combine? Which can you delegate? Cast a critical eye over your list as you consider these questions—and be realistic. Do you honestly think you are going to work on twelve different projects today? If so, you're probably stretching your time, and yourself, too thin. I recommend that you think through your list and edit it down to no more than four to six projects to make your plan more manageable, realistic, and achievable.

Giving yourself and your teammates much more than you will realistically accomplish may keep the pressure on, but remember this: the Aces succeeded in staying cool and making good decisions by learning to dial back the pressure. They concentrated each mission on attaining only a few critical goals. By keeping their mission tactics simple and focused on only the most important goals, the Aces almost always achieved great results. The legitimate confidence they developed through those successes helped them control their reactions and make good decisions under the severe pressures of combat. It sounds obvious, but that is how they became Aces. Your simple workplace checklist helps you avoid getting caught in the firestorm of a potentially disorganized, frustrating, anxiety-filled day. With realistic, written daily goals, you can keep your cool and turn in peak performance despite the severity of unexpected challenges and problems that explode in your workday, usually at the worst possible times.

Step 2: Rank Priorities Within the Plan

At TOPGUN, we often wonder how we can get everything done on the POD, even with a thirty-member staff of highly motivated aviators and a fifteen-hour workday. In spite of unexpected events and unavoidable delays, however, every day, more than 90 percent of POD events are completed to TOPGUN's high standard. Here is a simple technique that plays a huge part in that success rate—the second step in our daily action plan process.

Every morning, TOPGUN instructors establish priorities in the POD. Ranking the most important things first gives us a firm grip on our day right from the start. We want to make sure we tackle the most important items first so they are completed on time and to TOPGUN's high standards. This step is not about getting everything done every day. That's impossible. Instead, it's about getting the *right* things done every day. That outcome is not only possible, it's essential, and it comes from prioritizing your daily written action plan.

I recommend that you begin the prioritization by dividing the day's activities into three groups:

- **The A-Group**—The A-group consists of the most important things you can do today to generate cash flow or otherwise boost revenues. This group should include no more than three of your major projects, but the gauge for access to this group is this: if you could complete just one thing today, what would it be? The biggest revenue

generators with the soonest close dates get your immediate
attention.

- **The B-Group**—This group includes potentially excellent
  sources of future revenue that may one day graduate to
  your A-Group. B-Group projects have a longer shelf life
  than the A-Group and should consist of no more than
  three projects.

- **The C-Group**—This last group includes everything else
  you do at work—items that may or may not ever mature
  into B- or A-Group status. These items don't require the
  same focus and attention to detail that you give to items
  in the other groups, but they can't be ignored either. You
  might, for example, smell a potential deal or problem
  brewing with an item in the C-Group. With careful
  attention to the details of that item and some decisive
  action, you can head off a potential problem before it gets
  started or beat the competition to secure a profitable, yet
  unexpected, opportunity. It's the order in which you attend
  to these items that differs, not the level of attention you
  give them.

What priority system do you use? Do you even have a daily priority system? You should. Using a priority system can help you
make immediate improvements in your daily performance. Like
other elements of the Peak Performance Formula, the rapid pace
and fast-moving changes that dominate the workplace today make
prioritization more important than ever. If you haven't classified
your projects into groups, you won't know if you're spending time
unwisely on B-Group work with A-Group work on hold.

What *you* do every day and how effectively *you* do it is a constant
source of discussion by senior management. Your ability to prioritize daily tasks helps you increase your value proposition for your
company. Forget about the deals you closed last year, the projects
you completed last quarter, the awards you won last month. They
do not matter today. What matters is the value you create today—
a cold but true reality. The better you are at prioritizing your daily

activities, the better you will be at adding or creating value each day, every day—and the more valuable you become to your organization.

TOPGUN's system of prioritization has helped it increase its performance every year. While TOPGUN is constantly adjusting its tactics and curriculum to remain current with emerging threats and new technologies, what never changes is the program leaders' commitment to superior performance. Central to that performance is their ability to get the right things done at the right time. Daily prioritization can deliver the same results for you.

Step 3: Tackle Activities According to Priority

There's a lot on your plate today. Can you get it all done? Even with a prioritized action plan, you may start the day feeling queasy about the day's responsibilities. You're not alone. The Aces all started their days with the same anxious feelings. I had them in varying degrees for every one of my

USING A PRE-LAUNCH CHECKLIST

Many executives jump right into their workday and attack it. But is that a good strategy? Sure, you are busy immediately. But are you productive? You could be setting yourself—and your team—up for a helter-skelter, chaotic day, resulting in unnecessary tension, anxiety, and stress.

Take a lesson from the Aces. Just before going to their planes, they met in the briefing room with teammates for a final "macro review" of their mission and a last look at the big A-Group priorities essential for that mission to succeed. Try this technique. Before launching into your daily activities, do a final review of your prioritized daily action plan and make further adjustments to streamline your workday agenda.

170 combat missions. I also have had those same stomach-churning feelings before every one of the 1,200 speeches I've delivered in my career. I interpret these feelings of anticipation as a good sign. They indicate you are highly focused on the outcome. Your senses sharpen, and you're intent on doing a good job. Once you start working on the things you've identified as most important, those anxieties begin to lessen. This was true for me as a combat aviator, and it has been equally true during my years as a commercial real estate agent and professional speaker.

With different multifaceted projects and tight deadlines, it's easy to feel unsure about where to start. Your tension, anxiety, and stress rise, right along with your blood pressure. How can you possibly get everything done today? That prioritized plan you've learned to create helps you skip this drama and focus on the work before you. After you write and prioritize your daily action plan, you no longer have to decide what to do next. You have it right in front of you; you just have to work through your list.

Mark Twain once observed: "The secret of getting ahead is getting started. The secret of getting started is breaking your complex overwhelming tasks into small manageable tasks, and then starting on the first one." Most executives feel sharpest early in the morning. All the more reason to tackle the toughest A-Group projects first. Follow Twain's advice and convert the largest steps within those projects into little steps, and build positive workplace momentum as you progress. But above all, make sure you resist the temptation to focus on easy tasks. Sure, it feels good to breeze through easy items on your list, or even to rationalize that you're just warming up for the trickier jobs ahead. As at TOPGUN, achieving peak performance in any type of work involves getting the right things done at the right time. Tackle the most important things first. You can never tell when or for what reasons an immediate action item will pop up and require your undivided attention.

Also avoid the temptation of jumping into B-Group work before most of your A-Group work has been finished. This can be tough to do when you're constantly swamped with meetings, phone calls, emails, text messages, and questions from senior management. You may enjoy some of the B- and C-Group work, but don't allow it to distract you. Attend to your prioritized list. When you drift off-mark, you need to recognize it immediately. Keep your list of priorities nearby. It keeps you on track and serves as an indispensable tool for achieving peak performance under pressure. Your daily action plan will help you identify when you can make time for B-Group projects—an especially important benefit when those projects unexpectedly rise in importance and require immediate action.

When the pressure mounts and you begin to feel overwhelmed by the ever-growing number of tasks before you, remember this one simple phrase: *Take priority action now.* Avoid the urge to put off action until you feel in the mood to get started. That's a sure way to accomplish little. Take action now and get the job started. You will be amazed at how your motivation increases once you are under way.

Step 4: Review Your Progress

To prevent having to constantly react to unexpected situations, periodically do a quick, one-minute review of your daily action plan at intervals throughout your workday. The military calls these periodic reviews a *howgozit*, or a *Sitrep* (Situation Report), and they use them to assess what has happened in the mission compared to what was planned, and whether the plan needs adjustment to meet unexpected threats and new developments. The Aces knew that their success depended on a constant series of airborne adjustments. Should you make adjustments in your workday? Absolutely, if you want to achieve peak performance under pressure.

I recommend that you take time at noon for one of these brief reviews. Ask yourself: What have I accomplished so far? What adjustments must I make? What is doable in the afternoon? How am I doing with those A-Group priorities? How did I handle things requiring my immediate attention this morning? Were they A-, B-, or C-Group items? What about my management style with myself and others? Is my style proactive or reactive? Which style creates more tension, anxiety, and stress for me and my teammates? By following the steps, you'll reduce your reactive moments. This will be a welcome change for you and your teammates.

Now imagine this: It seems like lunch was just a few minutes ago, but you look up and notice it is almost dark outside. Where has the day gone? You have some evening family commitments and need to wrap up your workday. What is the last thing you do before leaving the office?

Here is a lesson from the instructors at TOPGUN. They take a final look at their now-completed POD to see how they did. What did they accomplish? What didn't get done? Why? What corrective action is required for the uncompleted tasks? Who has been assigned to take that action? Should it be delegated? How does this fit in with the next day's plans? The answers to these questions form the basis for tomorrow's daily action plan.

You can use this same technique to boost your performance. At or near the end of your workday, cross out what you accomplished from your daily action plan and reorder the rest to carry over for tomorrow. (Isn't it fun to check off those completed jobs? That's another reason why I like converting the big steps to little steps. They offer a chance to cross out more completed items.) Review what you had planned and compare it with what you actually did. How'd you do? This is your daily performance report card.

Planning for a Balanced Life

Keep in mind that peak performance is not about the quantity of work you do. It is about completing the right work at the right time. Anybody can be busy. What counts is your productivity.

This point resonated with the Aces. I know that when flying over enemy territory we were extremely busy in the cockpit, monitoring a steady flow of information pouring in from multiple sources. But we also had to be aware of what was happening outside the cockpit.

Otherwise, we could easily get shot down. Aces were always aware that when they had an enemy in their gun sight, they too could just as easily be in an enemy gun sight. The hunter is always being hunted.

Here's how this applies to your business. Consider those clients you've worked with for years. You've developed some long-term, profitable relationships. But your competitors are also regularly calling on these same customers. Your clients may be impressed with a competitor's pricing, account servicing, or money-back guarantees. Some clients may be considering a switch and terminating you, especially if their business has reorganized, been purchased, or merged with another company. If you're too busy being busy, or if you allow circumstances to guide your actions, rather than continually directing and measuring your progress against the tactical and strategic goals outlined in your organization's business plan, you may not have even an inkling of this gathering storm until it's too late. All it takes is the loss of a few key accounts or clients to throw you, your job, and your company upside down. If you aren't targeting your long-term goals and being smart and productive with your time, unnecessary distractions and busy-ness could cost you some long-standing, profitable client relationships.

While Ace fighter pilots and top-performing executives share many similarities, they also have critical differences. Aces became obsessed with their work as a matter of survival. Their lives and those of their teammates depended on achieving their goals, regardless of the circumstances. Business leaders operate with a different template. Despite workplace pressures, they don't put their lives at risk. They and their teammates will almost certainly survive the day and see their families at night.

This brings up an important point. You and your team all have lives away from your jobs. How do you live a balanced life in today's ever-more-demanding workplace? In short, you need to *plan* for a balanced life. Review your business plan regularly, and make sure that everyone on your team understands and is working toward its strategic, operational, and tactical goals. Take control of your day by creating and implementing a daily action plan. Arrive at work early, get a good fix on what's most important that day, work smart, and get those important things done earlier in the day, if possible.

And then, when it's time to go home, *go home.* Work will always expand to fill the amount of time you are willing to spend working. Turning into a workaholic is easy. But continually working late leads to unhealthy (and unnecessary) doses of daily tension, anxiety, and stress. That can leave you exhausted, irritable, short-tempered, and impatient. Moreover, if work is your sole focus in life, you won't have much of a life other than work. You may recognize these symptoms in someone you know. With this toxic mix of pressures bubbling away inside you at work and then at home, it is impossible to maximize peak performance under pressure. But it doesn't have to be that way. Planning is more than just the first element in the Peak Performance Formula; it's your strongest tool in taking control of your work. That frees up your time and attention so you can focus on all of the other important aspects of your life.

Chapter Debrief

Here are some questions to help you pull together your understanding of the ideas and information you've learned in this chapter:

Q} How effectively are you and your teammates utilizing the planning concepts introduced in this chapter? Would you rate your utilization of these planning concepts as *good, fair,* or *poor*? Why?

1. When was the last time you reviewed your organization's business plan? Are you happy with the plan? Why, or why not? What one thing would you like to immediately change to make the plan more effective?

2. Do you and your team have your own personal, written business plans? When was the last time you reviewed your business plan and those of your teammates?

3. Do you and your team have a full understanding of your organization's strategic, operational, and tactical plans? If asked, can you and your team explain your organization's plans? When was the last time you discussed them as a team? Do you ever ask your teammates for recommendations to make them better? Why, or why not?

4. Are all strategic, operational, and tactical plans clear, up to date, and easy to understand? How are they linked? Are these links supported by you and your team? Why, or why not?

Your response: _____

_____

_____

_____

Q} Are you and your teammates completing all assigned tasks and projects in the most professional manner possible on or before assigned completion dates? Why, or why not?

1. Is your team exceeding, meeting, or running behind its scheduled project deadlines? Why?

2. When were these deadlines last updated?

3. How realistic are they?

4. What do your teammates think of your planned goals and deadlines? Are these goals realistic? What recommendations have they made?

5. Do you listen to these recommendations? Why, or why not? What has to change for you to listen to teammates' inputs?

6. How often do you meet with your team to discuss these matters?

7. What changes can you implement now to make your plans immediately more effective?

Your response: _____

_____

_____

_____

Do you consistently get the most important things done each day at work? Are you starting your days working on the most important things first? Why, or why not? What has to change in order for you to start each day working on your most important jobs and projects?

1. Do you use a daily action plan? Why, or why not? What about your teammates—what do they use?

2. What is your process for prioritizing your day's activities? Does it work? How do you know? What can you do to make it work more effectively?

3. Do you complete most of the jobs you want to complete every day?

4. What's the biggest factor preventing you from completing each day's most important jobs? What's your solution? When will you implement it?

5. Are you typically busy or productive during your workday? Which is more effective? Why? What does your report card say?

Your response: _____

_____

_____

_____

Have you been able to strike a balance between your workplace requirements and your family commitments? What's the biggest obstacle to your finding this workplace–family balance?

1. Do you have sufficient time for family and friends? What has to change to provide you with more time for them? When will you make those changes?

Your response: _____

_____

_____

_____

CHAPTER THREE

PREPARING TO WIN

"It is not the strongest of the species that survive, nor the most intelligent, but the one most responsive to change."
—CHARLES DARWIN

Among their many strengths, the Aces had an uncanny ability to do two things exceptionally well: First, they recognized their opponents' mistakes and pounced on them to win. Second, they recognized their own mistakes and immediately took corrective action. How did the Aces learn to do these two things so well? The big-picture answer to that question is that, by mastering the same skills you are learning as elements in the Peak Performance Formula, they were able to dial back the pressures they faced and take quick, decisive action to deal effectively with the situation at hand. To put it more simply, the Aces managed to survive and win in the face of big challenges and escalating pressure *because they had prepared to do just that.*

The second element in the Peak Performance Formula, and one of the Aces' most powerful habits, is relentless preparation. It enabled the Aces to control their response to the highest levels of tension, anxiety, and stress of combat at the most critical times, and to react quickly in a dogfight, no matter what unexpected maneuvers their enemies might spring on them. As a result, Aces almost always made good decisions at critical times. Their fast-reaction flying came only after countless hours devoted to training for their missions and practicing their simple plans. The Aces left nothing to chance; they went into every battle prepared to win. Henry Ford once said: "If you think you can do it, you're right, you can; if you don't think you can do it, you're also right, you can't."

As I mentioned previously, many fighter pilots think that when they face their greatest pressures, they will somehow magically rise to the occasion, but they don't. Instead, they fall back on their level of training. That's why TOPGUN has always emphasized the importance of training hard and training realistically. It takes the right training, not luck, to survive in air combat. The Aces prepared to win by training doggedly, diligently, and realistically. TOPGUN's instructors continue this tradition by creating tough battle-related problems in training flights more severe than those their students might encounter in combat. I'm still incredibly grateful to my TOPGUN instructors, Pete (Viper) Pettigrew, Dave (Falcon) Frost, Dave (Bushwacker) Bjerke, and Jim (Hawkeye) Laing, for training me and my teammates so thoroughly. Everything Duke and I saw enemy planes do in combat, we already had seen in our TOPGUN training. Our final dogfight over North Vietnam against the enemy's leading Ace could have had a different outcome had we not been thoroughly prepared for just such a situation against superbly flown TOPGUN jets.

In business, as in combat, preparation is the critical foundation for all good decision making. Do you typically think you will always rise to the occasion during challenging times at work? That you will be able to wing it or go with your gut and still get by? Why on earth would you run the risk of falling short of your best performance during a time when you can least afford it? Instead, I recommend that you prepare for your workdays and your organization's success the way the Aces prepared for combat. For any competitor intent on winning, *the will to succeed is of little value without the will to prepare.*

You have heard the expression "Knowledge is power." Well, preparation is all about knowledge. In order to succeed in today's marketplace, you must have a clear understanding of your mission and goals, as well as a full knowledge of your business and industry, your marketplace trends, and the strengths and weaknesses of your competitors. You then must understand how these factors influence the challenges you are facing, how physically and mentally capable you are of meeting those challenges, and how well positioned you and your team are to win. In this chapter, we're going to take a close look at each of the five essential areas of preparation, along with some specific ideas for promoting success in each of them. You can use the techniques and tactics outlined in this chapter to develop your own program of *relentless preparation*. With that, you move one step closer to mastering the Peak Performance Formula *and* to becoming fully prepared to win in any area of competition.

Preparing to Compete: Know Your Mission

All preparations flow from your company's mission statement. In just one sentence, it tells your potential and existing customers what you do, why you are qualified to do it, and how they will benefit most by doing business with you. Think of the mission statement as your elevator pitch—the most compelling reasons for doing business with you that you could outline to a potential client during a short elevator ride. You have about seven seconds to make your pitch. To fit the bill, your mission statement has to be clear, concise, current, and ready to go anytime. Here, for example, is TOPGUN's mission statement: "To teach Navy and Marine fighter pilots how to put the right weapons on the right targets at the right time, no matter what."

What is *your* mission statement? If you don't have one, write one now. If you have one that isn't succinct or powerful or current, revise it to fit the seven-second elevator-pitch rule. Compose it in both business and personal terms. The time you spend working on your statement will have the additional benefit of helping to ground you in the reasons you are in business and the biggest benefits you bring to your work, customers, team, and company.

Preparing to Succeed: Know Your Business

This is the academic side of your job. You have to know your business before you can succeed at it. The more you know about your business, the better able you are to deal with its uncertainties. Consider the simple premise for Aces: fighter pilots surprised in combat are fighter pilots in trouble. This applies equally to executives on the job. Business executives surprised at work may also be business executives in trouble. To avoid these nasty surprises, you have to prepare yourself by learning all that you can about the business and industry in which you work.

Are you mentally prepared to win? Are you satisfied with how well you know the academic side of your job? Do you know all the details of your products and services? What else would you like to add to your quiver of academic arrows? To help build your business knowledge and become better prepared to leverage it, you should have at your fingertips well-thought-out answers to questions about your organization, such as:

- How is your product or service made or structured? How long does that process take? What is your contribution?

- What does each element of your product or service cost in time and money? What is your return on investment (ROI)?

- Where do you get your materials? With growing market emphasis on environmental issues and human rights, you need to have solid answers. Customers will ask. Competitors will tell them.

- Does your company need to change a vendor or personnel? What will that cost? What are the tradeoffs?

- Do you know how to use the latest technology available to your business or industry? If not, what are you doing about it? What new technologies will you introduce to help you and your team operate more effectively?

All of the Aces I interviewed shared a burning desire to increase their knowledge base. The reason was simple: the more they knew, the better they performed. They were aware of what they did *not* know and worked tirelessly to expand their knowledge and improve their performance in those areas. I recommend that you take a page from the Aces' training manual, and make a daily commitment to dig into the details of your own business or industry. Your goal, just like that of the Aces, is to be prepared to come out on top of your competitors who are aggressively hunting for the same prospects and clients you are pursuing.

Preparing for Risks: Know Your What-Ifs

The Aces knew from experience that most of their carefully thought-out plans didn't survive first enemy contact. They were acutely aware that in the heat of battle they would have no time to think through or analyze their predicament. In air combat, everything happens really fast. Surrounded in the surreal fog of war all too familiar to combat veterans, the Aces had to react immediately and adeptly, even as a flood of emotions raged through their bodies. To succeed, they needed an ironclad grasp of all the logical what-ifs—not just the potential events and outcomes of their next move, but the life-or-death what-ifs of a winner-take-all fight to the finish with no rules.

In a dogfight, you must review your options in a split second as you instantaneously analyze your enemy's options and predict his potential actions. Then it's on. You are immediately engaged in mortal combat, knowing full well that the fight you are in could unexpectedly end, for any participant, as quickly as it began. TOPGUN calls this type of split-second assessment and decision making "reaction flying." It's a fundamental point of emphasis during the TOPGUN course. The strength of an aviator's reaction flying is directly related to the strength of his or her preparation and, ultimately, performance.

Based on their relentless preparation, the Aces were able to quickly assess their enemy's chosen maneuvers as good, fair, or poor, and to respond appropriately. Like chess masters, the Aces pitted their strengths against their enemy's weaknesses, looking for mismatched situations to exploit. By thinking several moves ahead, Aces saw the whole problem. They were prepared for any contingency. They had thought about the many what-ifs of their mission and trained for it over many months. That's how they were able to instinctively and calmly shift mental gears during rapidly deteriorating flight conditions.

Now, instead of two fighter pilots engaged in a dogfight, consider a face-off between equally capable executives of rival corporations. Who do you think will win the competition if one is too busy to give much thought to planning the next move while the other is planning three moves ahead? To be the winner in your face-offs, against tough, well-qualified competitors, you need to use the what-if approach to preparation. This will enable you to anticipate and quickly handle most unplanned events that might arise. For example:

AVOIDING EMOTIONAL DECISIONS

Most fighter pilots viewed the enemy with hatred, contempt, and disgust. Although Aces harbored the same feelings, they were able to dial back these feelings. Why? They wanted to avoid the trap of making emotional—rather than rational—decisions during the strain of combat dogfights. Aviators who made emotional decisions in combat risked falling short in their mission goals. Emotional decisions sometimes cost pilots their lives. Those with a clinical, detached approach to decision making kept their cool and didn't choke. These aviators didn't make emotion-laced decisions under pressure or take unnecessary risks in the heat of battle.

Because they were able to tweak back those powerfully negative emotions common to all mortal combatants, they saved themselves a huge amount of tension, anxiety, and stress. This emotional control also paved the way for better relationships later in life. I have met German and Japanese Aces at American Fighter Aces reunions. Once I asked a Luftwaffe Ace, with thirty-eight shoot-downs, what he thought about socializing with his former enemies. He replied crisply in his German—English staccato: "This is great! I have much more in common with these people than I do with my own countrymen."

Success in today's economy demands rational, unemotional decisions. In competing head-to-head with other companies for the same clients or dealing with tough, pressurized work situations, roll back any negative feelings. They might be justified, but so what? Of greater importance is keeping your cool so you can achieve your ultimate goals.

- What if your company decides to merge several profit centers within your region? Could that mean a substantial employee downsize is looming? If so, what do you say to your staff?

- What if senior management plans to move a significant portion of your company's operation to another state, or even out of the country? What—if anything—should you say to your team?

- What if a new management group is about to take control of your department? That could mean a major change in job titles and executive assignments. How should you prepare for this?

- What if your boss needs to reduce your team by five members and still expects you to produce a 15 percent revenue increase? How should you respond?

- What if a major competitor offers your client of many years a

20 percent discount or free product delivery? What should you do?

- What if one of your top clients gets into financial trouble and cuts its order by 30 percent?

To prepare for any and all what-ifs, you need to study the issues and formulate well-thought-out responses. This is simple *contingency planning*. Perhaps you can't match the competitor's offer, but you may be able to present something else, such as a longer warranty or an earlier delivery date. Or, if your boss provides the latest account-management software for your team, you could expect to achieve an 18 percent annual increase in revenues. No matter what contingency you are considering, you must spend sufficient time with your team learning from your mistakes and discussing your what-if scenarios. Your goal is to be prepared to address the most likely customer and prospect objections. This is called simply *contingency planning*.

The Aces I interviewed always briefed their likely what-ifs before every mission. In my case, I went through those what-if briefings twice a day for seven months. The time and attention I invested in that preparation saved my life when we were in that burning, spinning, out-of-control jet over enemy territory. I had been reviewing and preparing for that very situation (including the out-of-control flight procedures) every day in training for almost two years before my first combat mission. When our plane was hit by that missile and we had to take decisive action to survive, our decisions were quick, instinctive, and successful.

If you use the what-if approach to prepare for the potential risks and upheavals in your daily business routine, you will raise your performance dramatically—whether or not those risks come to pass. You will also boost your credibility with clients. And when hard-hitting workplace problems erupt, you will have the opportunity to perform with distinction.

Today everybody is busy, overcommitted, and pressed for time. Being busy is easy—being productive is hard. You need to have a ready what-if response teed up to quickly address any unexpected

PREPARING YOUR TEAM FOR THE WHAT-IFS AHEAD

In my thirty-year career in commercial real estate, I used the what-if approach to relentlessly prepare for deal-associated risks with my teams and clients. We had consistently excellent results. We called what-if team meetings prior to getting together with clients, prospects, vendors, and senior management our "pre-meeting meeting." These pre-meetings were decisive in helping us achieve our goals during the actual business meetings. As a result, we were seldom surprised and always ready. Those across the table from us were sometimes surprised and never as well prepared. What about your seat at the negotiation table? Are you on the side that's best prepared? You can boost your chances of being on the winning side of most negotiations by making sure that both you *and* your team are fully prepared to tackle any what-if risks that might arise.

challenges head-on. A clumsy reply like "I'll get back to you later" or a beat-around-the-bush answer is not what your client, prospect, or boss wants to hear. But that's what happens when you arrive unprepared to work, in meetings, or on conference calls.

Clients don't care that your email is down, or you're having a tough day, or you're overscheduled, or you're coming down with a cold. When they deal with you, they want to know what's in it for them. They expect to know what you can do right now to help solve their problems or fill their needs. If you are unprepared to address their specific demands, you run the risk of giving answers that come across as weak and ineffective. Those kinds of answers erode your confidence and your credibility. Clients notice. They may not say anything about it to you directly, but later, they will say plenty to each other. Their topic: assessing all the pros and cons of doing business with you, your company, or your competitors.

Preparing for Peak Performance: Know Your Capabilities

There's an old saying that goes something like this: "When you feel better, you perform better. When you don't, you won't." That statement speaks to a core premise of relentless preparation. Whether you are flying a jet fighter in air combat or dealing with the challenges of your typical business day, the better you feel, the better you perform.

Let me explain the physical demands of flying today's jet fighter in high G-force dogfights. We expect the aviators we train at TOPGUN to fly their jets, as we say, "one inch from out of control at all times in a purposeful way." TOPGUN students fly twice a day, six days a week, for almost ten weeks. The airborne battle problems they must solve are tough and sophisticated and almost always involve unknown numbers of "enemy" airplanes flown by the TOPGUN instructors. This rigorous schedule requires top physical condition.

All dogfights are flown fast, typically at speeds from 400 mph to 650 mph. (The speed of sound, known as Mach 1.0, is 643 mph at sea level.) The instructors and students are constantly making hard rolling, or pitching, turns against each other at 6 Gs to 8 Gs. A 200-pound pilot making a 6-G turn has the equivalent of 1,200 pounds of pressure crushing down on him; at 8 Gs, the equivalent pressure goes up to 1,600 pounds. The following pictures show the effects of these forces on the human body.

Courtesy of the U.S. Air Force.

Handling high G-forces while flying your jet properly takes some getting used to. It also requires top physical condition. Sometimes it is a real strain to stay conscious during the high-G turns, which can take up to ten seconds to complete. For someone like me, in his mid-sixties, a ten-second 8-G turn can seem like ten minutes.

You may never experience elevated physical G-forces, but the emotional G-forces, which many of us encounter most days at work, can be just as difficult to withstand. Anyone dealing with today's overloaded workdays, uncertain job status, possible layoffs, company restructurings, and major management changes knows what I mean. And there may be a whole host of tough family issues in need of your immediate attention when you finally go home to unwind. But there's good news: the same basic techniques work for dealing with both types of G-forces, and those techniques revolve around good health habits.

To be prepared to respond rapidly, make good decisions, and maintain focus on your goals while paying attention to the many details of your mission, you need to stay on top of your physical condition. Every year, all naval aviators go through an extensive six-hour flight physical. Everything must check out near-perfect—otherwise we no longer can fly. Not surprisingly, your physical health plays a huge role in your ability to perform at your best as a leader and decision maker. At work, you're under a lot of pressure. In today's chaotic economy, you can expect that work is only going to get tougher and more challenging. A good friend who is a top cardiac surgeon in San Diego has told me many times: "Preventative medicine is always better than cure medicine."

I have been flying tactical Navy jet fighters for parts of the past six decades. I am very lucky. Today, at age sixty-five, I weigh the same as when I graduated from high school almost fifty years ago. (I can still wear the same suit I wore in high school.) My blood pressure is the same at age sixty-five (110/65) as when I joined the Navy at twenty-three. But good physical condition doesn't just happen. I prepare every day to make sure I can pass those six-hour annual flight physicals, endure high-G TOPGUN flights, and remain intently focused through twelve-hour workdays. I'm not writing a guide to physical conditioning here, but I do want to pass along some very basic ideas and techniques that you can consider as you form your own health-maintenance plan. That way, you'll be physically—as well as mentally—prepared to take on any workplace challenge.

We all have physical factors beyond our control, including the genes we inherited from our parents. So let's concentrate here on the things we *can* directly control: our diet, exercise, and rest.

Considering Your Diet

Let's begin with diet. I have always subscribed to the theory that you are what you eat. I also believe in one of the favorite sayings of our mothers, "Breakfast is the most important meal of the day." I travel the country as a professional speaker. Many of my morning venues begin after the breakfast buffet. There are usually 200 to 300 attendees. I notice that the fruit, cereal, and yogurt trays offered on the tables almost always remain full. The sweet rolls, sausage, bacon, eggs, and grits trays, on the other hand, are constantly being refilled. I think everyone in these rooms has heard the same advice I have heard—eat a good, healthy breakfast, but don't load up on excessive calories, fats, and carbs. Choosing to follow that advice, however, is an individual decision.

I follow a diet aimed at maximizing my physical health. Why put low-test fuel in your body when high-test is available? I avoid red meat, fried foods, fast foods, sweets, and soft drinks, choosing instead to eat fresh fish, vegetables, low-fat yogurt and other dairy, whole grains, green tea, and mineral water. I don't smoke or drink alcohol. I also read the labels on most packages. I never use salt on anything because so much of our food already contains substantial amounts of sodium. Please believe me: I am not trying to represent myself as an expert on nutrition. I only know what works for me.

The real question is, What works for you, and what changes can (and will) you make to prepare yourself to win? And where do you start? I recommend that you use a technique you are already familiar with from your project timelines: *If it's not measured, it's not managed.* Start by seeing your doctor. Get a full physical and note your weight and physical condition for your age group.

Each year, we make more than 1,800 eating decisions. This equates to approximately thirty-five eating decisions a week. I am the first to acknowledge that, on occasion, I slip up. But my slipups are short-lived. I try to get right back on track. I am well aware of the physical challenges that await me at TOPGUN and at work. And you, too, are well aware of the physical challenges that await you each day on the job. If you are serious about improving your performance at work under pressure, feeling better, and having more energy, make an honest review of your diet. What can you add or eliminate to improve your diet? Talk to your doctor or a sports nutritionist so you'll be assured you're using the most current information available to get the best results possible for your age, gender, and body type. See what kinds of healthy changes you can most easily incorporate quickly into your diet; then, as that famous advertisement advises, *just do it.*

Adding Exercise to Your Routine

In the sedentary conditions most of us work in today, exercise is as critical as diet in determining our physical and mental preparedness. Just as most doctors recommend, I try to do something physically demanding almost every day. For me, it's like taking out the emotional trash. We all deal with packed schedules. Finding the time to work out is always a challenge. Here are just a few ideas that work for me:

- **A regular schedule makes workouts more likely to happen.** If I wait for some free time to open up during the workday, I probably won't work out.

- **The earlier in the day, the better.** I lay out my workout clothes the night before, so all I have to do is get up, get in them, and get going.

- **Mood has nothing to do with it.** I never wait until I'm in the mood to work out. If I did, I probably wouldn't get much exercise. Once under way, I'm happy to be working out.

- **My workout is part of my essential preparation.** I'm serious about my workouts. I don't allow phone calls, emails, text messages, or unexpected visitors to interfere.

Now, enough about me. I'm not a professional trainer, but I know that everyone can find some way to benefit from regular exercise. Remember, doing something is better than doing nothing. Even a walk around the block is a start. And you should also bear in mind that when you miss a day's workout, you've missed it—period. You can't get it back by doing a double workout the next day. (Who has time for that anyway?)

Whatever you do, realize that the benefits of exercise aren't just reflected in the mirror; your physical condition makes a real difference in your ability to maximize your performance in every aspect of your personal and professional lives. You too have a relentless barrage of emotional Gs waiting to smack you in the face every day at work. If you're serious about maximizing your energy level at work, choose a few exercise action items and implement them immediately. You'll empty your emotional trash, more clearly see your daily priorities, and feel calmer and more confident as you move through your day. Try it. You'll be pleased with the results.

Guarding Your Rest

This brings us to the final component of the physical preparation of Aces: rest.

Rest may be the most important element of your physical and mental preparation. We are all familiar with hectic twelve-hour workdays, weekend work, unforeseen problems, tight deadlines, phone calls, emails, performance expectations, meetings, crisis management, layoffs, downsizing, rightsizing, more emails, new technologies, formal presentations, more meetings, relentless competition, and yet more emails—the building blocks, in other words, of a 24/7 no-life work schedule. And then there's the time we want *and need* to spend with our family and friends.

Something has to give, and too often, we wind up cutting back on our sleep time. That can be a big mistake. Numerous recent studies on the consequences of sleep deprivation in the workplace all agree that without proper sleep, your performance on the job could be compromised by:

- Poor concentration
- Poor decision making
- Irritability
- Poor memory function
- Slower reaction times
- Excessive impatience

We can be well intentioned with a commitment to proper diet and exercise programs. Without proper rest, however, we eliminate more than 30 percent of the feel-better-perform-better equation. Once fatigue, lack of energy, and exhaustion become our daily companions, those well-intended diet and exercise programs fall by the wayside.

Experts usually recommend eight hours of sleep per night, although individual needs range anywhere from six to ten hours. According to the National Sleep Association, a not-for-profit education organization in Washington, DC:

- Americans are sleeping 1.5 hours less per night than we did twenty years ago. That's more than three weeks of lost sleep per year.
- More than 47 million of us do not get enough sleep.
- More than 30 million report problems with insomnia.

- Approximately 40 million report waking up several times per night. Two-thirds of this group, more than 30 million of us, cannot get back to sleep.

- One of the leading causes of the above sleep problems? You guessed it: work-related stress.

So how are we supposed to maximize our performance at work when we're sleep deprived? If you have severe sleep-related problems, see your doctor. He or she can recommend a number of methods for improving your ability to sleep. Here are some of those recommendations, along with a few of my own:

- Regulate what and when you eat. I typically eat a light dinner about three hours before bedtime. If I get hungry later, I reach for some fruit.

- Limit your screen-time (TV, computer, and smartphone) in the hours before you retire. What works for me: no emails, cell phones, or computer work after 7:00 p.m. Things will survive till the morning.

- Limit caffeine and alcohol consumption. I make it habit to have no caffeine after noon.

- Avoid sweets and sugar after 5:00 p.m.

- Regulate bedroom temperature and other environmental conditions. Many sleep experts recommend a cool bedroom and warm feet for a good night's rest.

Sleep experts tell us that preparation for a good night's sleep begins right after you get up in the morning. If the ideas I've listed above don't sound like fun, remember how you feel in the middle of the night, wide awake, and worried about the upcoming day. That's no fun either.

Again, I'm not a doctor, a dietician, or a fitness coach. I simply know that physical condition plays a tremendous role in the ability to perform well at *any* task under pressure. As a result, I have made a lifelong commitment to proper diet, exercise, and rest. If you make that commitment, you too can experience a big improvement in your health—and your on-the-job performance.

Preparing to Lead: Know Your Team

In the Navy, aircraft carrier commanding officers, called captains, are consummate leaders who have prepared throughout their careers for the responsibilities of leadership. Aircraft carriers are floating cities, home to more than 5,500 sailors. During flight operations, these sailors work eighteen-hour days, seven days a week, for two to three weeks straight, for below minimum wage. Yet most are highly motivated and would do just about anything for their captains. How do these captains motivate their crews to work such long, hard hours for such little pay? Although most captains graduate with honors from our nation's finest universities, their leadership training extends well beyond the limits of formal schooling. And among the most important leadership principles Navy captains master is this one: *People really are a leader's biggest asset.* This principle represents a core belief in naval culture that dates back to the founding of the U.S. Navy, more than 230 years ago. In the course of their careers, each of these captains has witnessed the successes of those who follow this principle and the failures of those who ignore it. Numerous businesses and organizations today are quick to stake a claim to this same idea. In truth, however, few truly commit to it.

Human nature is the same whether you command an aircraft carrier, run a business, or lead your team at work. The people who depend on you every day—clients, prospects, colleagues, senior management, and subordinates—all consider three critical questions when they evaluate your ability to lead them and their willingness to follow you. Just as a ship's captain must answer to his or her crew, your success as a leader depends on your reply to those same three questions. Let's review each of them.

Question 1: Do You Know Me?

How well do you know the people you work with every day? When I am scheduled to give a presentation before a company or organization, I prepare by learning everything I can about the company's chief executive officer. I call his or her assistant in advance and ask questions about the CEO's full name, date of birth, hometown, brothers, sisters, spouse, children, favorite sports team, books, hobbies, and so on. I try to gather as much background information on the individual as possible.

During my presentation in front of the company, when I talk about team leadership and how this question—*Do you know me?*—relates to them, I'm already off the stage and positioned close to the CEO. I smile politely at the audience and tell them what this question means to me. I then recite all the information I've learned about their leader. The audiences and CEOs are amused, and sure, I'm using an extreme example of knowing someone's background. But I use this technique to illustrate an important people skill. Hidden in that CEO's background are some real gold nuggets of interest that he or she might love to talk about, if asked. Most people like to be known and understood by those around them—particularly by those who are leading

PROFILING THE ACES

The Aces I interviewed are at the very top of the world's most exclusive aviation club. The United States has 310 million people, compared with approximately 150 living American fighter Aces in 2012. Aces aren't like other fighter pilots, for several reasons. Here are just a few of the commonalities I found among this outstanding group of aviators:

- Almost all twenty-six Aces I interviewed were obsessed with fitness and exercised regularly. Most weigh about the same today as when they were flying, more than sixty to seventy years ago.

- They were delightful, funny people, quick to laugh—most heartily at themselves.

- All had been married, one at the age of seventy-six; none had been divorced; and almost 50 percent of them had been married to the same spouse for sixty or more years.

them. The human connection is powerful. If you want your people to know you, trust you, and be aware of what you expect from them, you first need to make the effort to know them and to let them know what they can expect from *you*.

If you feel you're too busy for the two-way process of getting to know your team (or you're simply uninterested in it), I ask you to stop for a moment and reconsider. As I noted earlier, whatever your occupational field, you are first and foremost in the people-influencing business. Think of this exercise as a great opportunity to take a giant step forward in advancing your people skills—and, believe me, *everybody notices*. Navy captains never miss any of these opportunities, nor should you. If you are wondering how to learn about the interests and experiences of the people on your team, here's a simple technique: *Just ask!*

Asking chatty questions and sharing anecdotes serve as a great way to set the table before the tough discussions begin. As we know, many events and meetings at work

- They arranged regular vacations, often to unusual places, and exciting adventures.
- Alcohol had been a problem for ten—as it was at one time for me—but each had been able to stop drinking.
- Most had smoked at one time, but all had quit or greatly reduced the habit.
- All refused to take foolish risks.
- All invested themselves in intensive preparation. When they flew combat, for example, they spent hours polishing each machine gun bullet and their guns, knowing that a jammed bullet or gun in a combat dogfight meant certain death.

The strong physical condition and upbeat attitude of these Aces helped them deal with life's other adversities, such as financial setbacks, the death of a loved one, and life-threatening illness.

are characterized by blunt talk. If you'd like a better chance to get more of what you need at work when those discussions occur, start by having your people briefly talk about themselves. You'll have to ask them, but the rest is easy. (Everyone is their own favorite topic of conversation.) Ask about their interests. Encourage them to tell you about their families, what they did over the weekend, or their kid's soccer team. When they talk, *listen!* Ask relevant questions. *Listen some more.*

If you know and are interested in your teammates and people at work, there's a good chance they're going to want to know and be interested in you. Of course, captains don't know detailed information about all 5,500 of their crew. But they know a remarkable number of names, hometowns, and job descriptions. And they're all exceptional listeners, a trait also mastered by top-performing executives. When flight operations are secured, many times the captains are out mingling with the crew. They do this because they know they'll push everyone hard when flight operations resume. And these walk-and-talks provide the captain with a golden opportunity to articulate the importance of the carrier's mission that day to small groups of the crew. They're also a great way to find out what's really happening on the ship. It sure beats reading a report. These conversations aren't about being popular or well liked; they're about earning the crew's respect. The time you spend learning about and listening to your team sends them an important message: *The boss is interested in me and what I do.* If you're serious about earning the respect of your people, take that first step. Get to know them.

Captains also know that the respect they need to command their ship must be earned, and re-earned, every day. They can't rest on their laurels. The respect you enjoy at work doesn't come as a result of your title; it comes from how your team perceives you as a leader. The time you spend with your team can help assure them that you *do* know them and care about their issues and interests. And that type of connection pays big dividends when your team is called into action.

Question 2: Do You Care About Me?

I believe in the saying "Real leadership comes from the heart, not the head." By getting to know your team, you're showing them that you care about them. That's a first step in getting your team to care about you and your goals for the team. This is not about sucking up or layering on the fake sincerity for your own gain. Sailors can quickly spot a phony. So can the people you deal with every day.

Here's another point worth considering: A good leader inspires others with confidence in him or her. A *great* leader inspires others with confidence in themselves. Do you inspire that kind of self-confidence in those you work with by showing them that you care about their goals, their situations, and the obstacles they are facing? Before answering, consider the following scenarios:

- You meet a senior executive or your new department head for the first time. He or she gives you a cheerful yearbook smile and tells you how great it is to meet you—right before calling you by the wrong name.

- As you meet colleagues in a room full of senior company executives, they tell you how *delighted* they are to see you, but they're not looking at you when they shake your hand. They're checking around the room to see who else more senior is available to schmooze.

- You finally get a few minutes with a colleague you have tried to track down all morning. You start to explain your concerns over an issue when your colleague's cell phone rings. Your colleague informs you the call is important and walks away.

- You're conducting a meeting with a group of executives from different departments in preparation for an important client presentation later that week. Several executives, with major roles in the presentation, are sending emails and texting.

Would you feel inspired or valued by any of this behavior? Of course not! These kinds of brush-offs would leave anyone feeling unimportant, insignificant, and of little value to the people they work for and with. Unfortunately, this obvious lack of interest is common in the workplace, and it can create a bad impression that spreads rapidly. As I mentioned before, really listening to others and demonstrating that you care about what they are saying is a critical skill for leaders, decision makers, and anyone who is committed to personal and professional success. But following up—checking on the status of problems or new initiatives, taking others' suggestions and ideas, congratulating them on successes, encouraging them to keep working toward their goals—is equally important.

In today's digital world, if you offend someone or make a mistake, within the hour their socially networked friends will have a posting of all the details. If you think it simply doesn't matter whether your team thinks you care about them, remember this: it's impossible to have teammates care about you and what's important to you at work until you first send a clear message that you care about them and what's important to them. If your people care about you, they'll help you get more of what you want, when you need it, during difficult times at work. And it's wise to have advocates in place before you need them.

Demonstrating to your team that you respect and care about them, their ideas, input, and workplace satisfaction is a major component of the second fundamental leadership principle: *If you care about those you lead, they will care about you.* A popular expression sums up this point: "People don't care how much you know until they first know how much you care." Embrace this principle, and you will have many supporters at work. Ignore it, and you risk having many detractors.

Question 3: Are You Willing to Help Me Get Better?

This question has the same value for any leader. For those who answer it positively, it has enormous potential for payback. Those aircraft carrier captains know that *they* benefit when their crew members get better at their jobs. The captain runs a tighter ship, and the crew operates more effectively, feels more confident, and is more productive. You can achieve the same benefits with your team members.

When you help any individual team member improve his or her performance, you boost the entire team's performance. It's a win-win.

Aircraft carrier captains use a very simple but effective method for helping their crew members improve their performance. Here's how they do it: Every ship operates like a city with departments—medical, legal, administration, accounting, and so on—run by a trained workforce. Even the kitchens—called "wardrooms" in the Navy—are well staffed. They have to be; any disruption in kitchen operations, however slight, sends a huge ripple of discontent around the ship. To keep on top of this operation, and to help boost crew members' performance, the captain makes random visits around the ship, which aren't random at all—they are planned in advance with senior department heads. During these visits, the captain takes time to talk to individual crew members, always inquiring about what help they need to improve their professional skills, education, and work environment. The captain asks these individuals questions such as:

- How's the job going today?
- Are you getting the support you need?
- What do you require that you don't have now?
- What can I do to help you?
- When's your next promotion exam?
- Have you completed all your practice exams? Need any help preparing?
- What are your career plans?

Questions like these help the captain understand his or her crew members' challenges and job effectiveness. That way, the captain can carefully gauge the readiness of the *entire* crew for doing the best possible work. In effect, leaders in any setting gain real benefits by helping their team members improve in their own work performance. As a leader, if you are willing to help your team members get better, they *will* get better. And that will help you.

So how do you help your people get better? Keep an ever-sharp eye out for professional development conferences, advanced degree programs, seminars, workshops, industry conventions, and the latest professional publications. As a professional speaker, I can attest to the wide variety of training opportunities available in today's economy. They run the full spectrum of value from barely average to outstanding. If I were paying for this training, I'd want to have several strong referrals from trusted sources and a firsthand look at the presenter in front of a group similar to my team. And, like an aircraft carrier captain, ask your team members what kinds of career or performance-boosting help they need. Here are examples of questions to ask your people if you're serious about helping them improve their professional skills:

- Are you satisfied with the software and computers we're using? Or do we need to upgrade? If so, what do you recommend?

- What type of computer training would be most helpful for you?

- Would you be interested in a time-management speaker at our next regional meeting? What other type of speaker would you recommend?

- There is a three-day professional selling skills course offered at the nearby college. Would you like to attend?

- Have you thought about getting your master's degree?

With today's constrained budgets and all expenses undergoing closer scrutiny, it's easy to ignore or dismiss the idea of spending the money to train your people. Or you may be worried that some could be lured away by a competitor and take your investment in their training with them. But do you really want to risk leading a team of unmotivated, poorly trained people? Do you think they're interested in turning in peak performance? I once heard the motivational speaker Zig Ziglar offer some great advice. He said that leaders shouldn't worry about training their people and losing them. Instead, they should worry about *not* training their people and *keeping* them.

Making the Connection

Just like the captains of huge aircraft carriers, you can't be everywhere at the same time. But, on a daily basis, you have an opportunity to make real and meaningful contact with a number of the people who work with you. You have the same opportunities as these captains every day to tell your people about:

- The importance and priority of your projects
- How your teammates fit into those projects
- The value each teammate brings to your team

Your benefit from this approach is that the more your people understand the importance of your projects and how they fit into project success, the more effectively they can execute your project plans.

You may still doubt what might appear to be a touchy-feely approach to leadership. But if you ever stood on a carrier deck at night during flight operations, you'd hear jet engines roaring so loud you can feel your heart vibrating against your rib cage. It's gritty, dangerous work done at night with lights out by hundreds of teammates as part of a precisely choreographed minuet of forty jet fighters. You'd quickly conclude there is nothing touchy-feely about this work, the people who do it, or their leaders.

Those leaders must be onto something special to get so many people to work so long and hard for so little pay and produce such remarkable results. That *something special* involves nothing more complicated than remembering the three important questions we've just reviewed. Considering those questions and developing your answers to them can help you build the same level of connection with your team that these Navy captains have with their crews. And that is a crucial first step *you* can use to prepare yourself and your team for achieving peak performance in every mission you undertake.

Chapter Debrief

How well prepared are you to succeed and lead in your workplace? To better understand your response to that question, and the information you've learned in this chapter, consider your answers to these questions:

Q} In one sentence, write out your company's mission statement. Are you satisfied with this statement?

1. How would you change your company's mission statement to make it more effective? Does your organization follow it closely at all times, sometimes, or not at all? Why, or why not?

2. Do you have a personal mission statement? If not, when will you create one? What will it contain? When was it last updated?

3. Write out your personal mission statement if you have one. Are you satisfied with your personal statement? What changes should you implement to make your personal mission statement more effective?

Your response: _____
_____
_____
_____

Q} How well do you know the strengths and weaknesses of your major competitors?

1. Is your information about your competitors current and accurate? How do you know? When was this information last updated? Who updated it?

2. What level of business and cost of products and services are your competitors providing? What do their deals look like? How do they compare with your company's products, services, and costs?

3. What sets you apart from the competition? What is your value proposition?

4. What makes you better than your competitors? Why are you different?

Your response: _____

_____

_____

_____

Q} How do you and your teammates prepare for each day's biggest challenges at work? Is your preparation strategy working? Why, or why not?

1. Are you prepared each morning to deal with all of the likely events or outcomes that might occur in your workday?

2. Do you and your team regularly review the potential roadblocks, pitfalls, and other risks that you might encounter in your workday?

3. Do you formulate well-thought-out responses to the tough issues or questions that might arise as you undertake new projects or meet with new prospects?

4. Do you work with your team to review mistakes and to consider numerous what-if scenarios associated with your operation?

Your response: _____

_____

_____

_____

Q} How would you evaluate your performance during times of great pressure at work? Do you perform well? Why, or why not? What one change would you have to make to improve your performance under pressure?

1. Do you feel physically and mentally prepared to be a successful decision maker?

2. When was the last time you had a physical? How's your physical condition? What's the easiest thing you can do to improve it? What's the most important thing you can do right now to feel better physically? When do you plan to take action?

3. Are you satisfied with your current diet? If not, how can you improve it? When are you going to start?

4. What one ten-minute physical activity or exercise could you add to your current schedule?

5. Do you get enough good, uninterrupted sleep? How much sleep do you need to perform at your optimum level? How would your doctor answer this question?

6. Do you answer email or update your social media communications each night before you go to bed? If so, do you think the benefits of doing so outweigh the costs of sound, restful sleep?

Your response: _____

_____

_____

_____

Q } When you make a blunt, honest assessment of your performance at work, do you think your teammates and senior management like working with you? Why, or why not?

1. Do you treat your team with respect? Do your actions demonstrate that you know them, care about them, and want to help them improve their performance?

2. What one activity could you add to your daily routine that would help increase your effectiveness as a team leader?

3. When was the last time you asked one of your team members about their day, and then really *listened* to their answer? How did you demonstrate that you were listening and heard what they had to say?

4. Do you ask about the family and children of your teammates? When was the last time you did this?

5. Do you like the people you work with? Why, or why not? Do you think they all like working with you? Why, or why not? What can you do to improve your work environment?

6. What can you do to improve your likability index with teammates and senior management?

Your response: _____

_____

_____

_____

CHAPTER FOUR

MAINTAINING FOCUS

*"Concentrate all your thoughts upon
the work at hand. The sun's rays do
not burn until brought to a focus."*

—ALEXANDER GRAHAM BELL

During my final combat mission, I was filled with raging feelings of tension, anxiety, stress, and fear—feelings I would never wish on anyone. As we started our climb for home, what we had just done began to sink in. Despite being badly outnumbered, Duke and I had shot down three enemy jets. In our final dogfight, we defeated an aggressive, skilled adversary in a harrowing, twisting, rolling duel in the sky. We had survived against incredible odds, and the sheer joy and relief of that knowledge washed over us like a waterfall. But that tiny moment of distracted celebration nearly cost us our lives. We were still forty miles inside enemy territory, which was no place to relax our focus.

As I described in the introduction, as we were congratulating each other, we saw several enemy jets circling over the treetops below, but so what? We thought they didn't see us, so we paid them no further attention. What a terrible blunder! Of course, those enemy MIGs could see our big Phantom, belching a stream of black exhaust against a hazy, pale blue sky.

For all 169 of our previous combat missions over the prior seven months, our focus had always been razor sharp. We were well trained and knew what to do. Our TOPGUN training before this combat deployment gave us the tools necessary to cope with our fear and other wide-ranging emotions. Our loss of focus during the last part of our final mission was simply a huge mistake—the very type of distracted thinking that can shoot down decision makers in *any* arena. That's why the ability to maintain sharp focus, particularly during challenging times, is an essential skill in all lines of work.

Any athlete can tell you about the important role of sharp focus in a winning performance. Consider, for example, the downhill giant slalom ski events at the Winter Olympics. Marvelously conditioned skiers in slick, skin-tight suits tuck into an aerodynamic posture and plunge down the slopes at up to 90 mph for 1.7 miles around poles laid out strategically to challenge speed and dexterity. These skiers shift their center of gravity rapidly left and right to clear each new pole, speeding on the very edge of control but still somehow maintaining their balance. Any mistake might end their run with a spectacular fall. Most world-class skiers have suffered broken arms or legs in high-speed spills and have had to work months at painful rehab to return to Olympic-caliber condition. They have to repair themselves mentally as well, to overcome their fear of taking another painful and costly fall, so they can focus on achieving peak performance. These athletes know that a few hundredths of a second can mean the difference between winning an Olympic gold, silver, or bronze medal—or not winning at all.

At the 2010 Winter Olympics, I watched a number of gold medal–winning skiers all say the same thing when asked how they did it. They attributed their winning runs to their ability to summon their highest level of focus and maintain it throughout the entire race. To them, that intense focus was the critical difference that separated them from their competition. As in so many competitions, most Olympic athletes are capable of winning, but those who are able to maintain the greatest focus for the longest period take the gold medal.

In this chapter, we're going to talk about focus, its role in the Peak Performance Formula, and how it impacts your performance at work. As you will learn, when I talk about focus, I mean your ability to pay attention to the right things at the right time, to concentrate, and to get into the right mindset for the many different and evolving work challenges you face in any given day. This chapter offers some ideas you can use to strengthen your ability to focus, drawn from the techniques used by the Aces to stay on top of events with their A-game intact, during the nerve-wracking chaos of combat. I'll show you how to use these same methods to maintain strong focus and to ramp it up to even greater levels of intensity when you need it most. You will learn how to zero in on the things that you *must* focus on at any given time and manage the details that will have the most impact on your outcomes. As a leader, your team members will always demand your attention. And so, the chapter will close with some ideas for how to most effectively focus your efforts on their concerns, challenges, and successes so you can maximize their performance and *your* results.

Developing Laser-Beam Focus in Three Essential Steps

During the past thirty years of serving as a TOPGUN instructor, a business executive, and a leadership consultant, I've seen plenty of evidence that focus is essential for success in any field or undertaking. I also am aware that the consequences of losing your focus vary a great deal, depending on your line of work, whether you're running your department or flying air combat. On the job, we want to successfully complete a project, win new business with an important client, or close a big deal. If we don't initially succeed, we learn from our mistakes, adjust, and get back out there tomorrow. If the Aces dropped their focus, even for a moment, they were done. For that simple reason, the Aces trained constantly to develop and maintain laser-beam focus and attention to detail. As a result, they missed almost nothing in those air battles and responded brilliantly to the many chaotic and unpredictable events exploding around them at any time. While learning to maintain that kind of focus takes commitment and experience, the Aces' approach was made up of three easy-to-implement steps:

1. Take on the right tasks at the right time.

2. Direct your attention to the most important issues/events occurring at any given moment.

3. Target your decisions/actions to have the greatest impact on essential outcomes.

Now let's take a closer look at each of these steps, and how you can use them to develop the finely tuned focus you need to maintain in order to perform at your best in any situation.

Step 1: Take on the Right Tasks at the Right Time

In their dogfights, the Aces had to know how to fly the right maneuvers and when to use them. When they flew combat, the Aces had to train their attention on any number of fast-emerging, life-or-death details. But at all times, they remained highly focused on the single most important task before them: winning. Their tactical decisions centered around two critical questions: what to do, and when to do it.

So how does this apply to your level of focus on the job at decision time? At work, most decision makers have to deal with a wide range of complex issues that bombard them from every direction. Deciding which tasks to tackle at what time is, therefore, the first skill you have to develop in order to become better at maintaining focus and making the right decisions. Where do you begin? Identify the most important issues demanding your attention—start there. Then, ignore or delegate anything that doesn't require your immediate attention. That's easily said, but doing it requires a system.

In choosing the right projects and times to ramp up your focus, your goal is to best position yourself for peak performance. The Aces knew that timing was critical to mission success and that the first element of preparedness was choosing the right time to take on the important tasks involved in their mission. That's a lesson you can learn from the Aces. Analyze your performance throughout the day to determine when your focus is sharpest and what type of environment helps you hone your attention and raise your concentration at work. By timing your most demanding or critical activities to fall within your peak performance zone, you'll find that you make better decisions. You also will accomplish more in less time—another factor that can help maximize your peak performance under pressure.

In the previous chapter, I recommended that you divide your daily activities into three groups, according to their importance, and tackle the most important group first. Many decision makers find great value in getting their day under way with the A-Group projects, rather than wasting time on easy tasks. That's a wise decision supported by many time-management experts. As you are working on these A-level jobs, two or three unexpected issues requiring your immediate attention are sure to crop up. If your peak performance zone occurs early in the day—as it does for most people—discipline yourself to stay on track with those A-level jobs. Save routine tasks for later, so that these interruptions won't keep you from accomplishing the things you *must* do on any given day.

As you work through important tasks or projects, you also can expect that more challenging aspects of that work may occur late in the process. The Aces knew they needed their most intense focus when the dogfight's outcome was imminent. They also were aware that the bigger the stakes—in their case, that win-or-lose moment—the greater the need for the highest focus. That's a good point for you to bear in mind as well.

The Aces were acutely aware of the consequences based on what they did *next*. As Duke and I learned when we got blasted out of the sky by that missile, focusing on past successes won't help you deal with rapidly developing new problems. No matter what kinds of obstacles or distractions present themselves, you have to keep moving your important projects ahead, and you cannot afford to let your focus waver as you near the end. Whether you are putting the final touches on a major client presentation or making a decision to avoid a delay triggered by a last-minute development, you can't afford to pull back on the throttle as you approach the finish line. Rather, light those focus-afterburners, suck it up, pay closer attention, and finish strong.

To help maintain your focus and attention to detail, no matter what last-minute issues arise, try invoking the 80/20 rule. Among other things, this rule tells us that 80 percent of essential activities in any process will take place during the last 20 percent of the job's timeline. By sharpening your focus during the final stages of your important tasks, you will be better able to shift resources, change operatives, add or delete steps, or otherwise respond effectively

A SIMPLE PLAN FOR IMPROVING YOUR FOCUS

My late father worked backbreaking construction during the mid-1930s Great Depression, an era of ten-hour workdays, six days a week, for seventy-five cents a day. For every job opening, 100 able-bodied laborers were ready to grab it. Before I started my first summer construction job, Dad told me that when he was a young construction worker, the foremen regularly fired men late in the day when they were tired and inclined to slack off. He told me to get to work early, keep my mind on my job, and work the hardest in that last hour, when everyone else was letting up. His advice proved invaluable. It applied equally to finishing a tough dogfight, closing a complex deal, or completing a demanding day at work.

So how can you stay focused when unexpected obstacles crop up just as you're about to wrap up a project? Here are a few simple suggestions: First, think about all the hard work that got you to this point, all of which has positioned you for a successful outcome. I am not suggesting that you drop off into a lengthy daydream about past successes; it only takes a moment to remind yourself that your training and preparation have enabled you to handle last-minute challenges and that you have done so many times in the past with excellent results.

As a professional speaker, that's how I deal with my pre-talk jitters, before walking out on the stage in front of 500 people to give a fifty-minute speech with no notes. I think about all the time I spent on those senior executive interviews, the company research, the countless hours organizing, creating, editing, finalizing, and practicing the speech. I walk out there knowing I've spent about one hour of preparation time for every minute of the speech. I'm ready, and I know it. But what about you? How do you make sure you'll have a strong finish for those big events and projects at work?

Here's my recommendation: when work gets wild and crazy (as it always does), take a brief break. Don't view this as dropping your focus, but simply as taking a moment to clear your head so you can focus even more intently on the details surrounding your task. Stand up. Walk around. Take a drink of water. Inhale, then slowly exhale through a few slow, deep breaths. Think about staying calm. Remember all the work you've done to get to this point. Recall your work with the what-ifs. In the past, you've dealt with situations just as tough as this, maybe even tougher. And you handled them well. Now return to your desk and give it your best shot.

to emerging problems professionally. Treat the last 20 percent as the most critical stage of your project's timeline. Then it will be easier to maintain a laser-beam focus while confidently making the last-minute decisions necessary to achieve maximum results.

I also recommend that you remember another important rule that I am sure you have seen proven time and time again: whatever can go wrong will—usually at the worst possible time. Yes, that's Murphy's Law, and it has a lot to teach us about maintaining unwavering attention to the details of our work. Whenever your workday seems to be totally under control and on track to achieve a predictable conclusion, you need to bring your attention into particularly sharp focus. Don't get complacent! What are the potential problem areas that could abruptly derail your seemingly smooth-flowing day? How do you plan to resolve them? What could you have done to avoid or reduce them altogether?

Here's the point: tackling the right job at the right time means learning to maintain your focus at all critical junctures in any task. Just like the Aces, you need to focus on being focused during those times. Choose the most important tasks, tackle them when your focus and attention are strongest, and then be sure to keep your focus trained on the details right up to the end.

Step 2: Direct Your Attention to the Most Important Issue/Event

Business consultants tell us that, in a typical year, approximately 25 percent of a company's clients account for all of its revenue. During that year, the company will lose about 5 percent of its existing customers while adding to its customer base by around 5 percent. And about 70 percent represent prospects, as shown in the pie chart below.

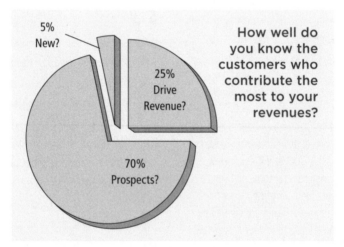

These new customers or clients don't just miraculously appear before you; they come from your company's prospect base. That means that someone in your company must first locate these people or organizations, then cultivate them as prospects, and then convince them to become clients. If you are a decision maker charged with making the deal, you will need to establish a relationship with these prospects. To keep clients you have landed, you will need to develop and continually nourish that relationship.

First, consider your new customers. How would you answer the following questions?

- How did you locate these new customers? What method worked best?

- How long did it take and how much did it cost you in time and capital to convince these prospects to become clients? What marketing techniques worked most effectively? Why?

- What other of your company's products or services might be of value to your new customers?

- Are there other products or services not yet created or available that might be valuable for these clients? What action will you take? When?

- How would you rank these new clients in your entire customer base, in terms of potential revenue? Number one? Top three? Top five? Other? These rankings will help you further focus your customer-interface lens.

- How do you plan to keep these new clients loyal to you?

- What is your "keep them sold" plan?

Remember that every new customer has something to teach you about your organization, your mission, your operation, and your performance. By targeting your focus on these clients, you can leverage those successes to broaden and deepen your customer relationships. You'll also find new ways to boost your personal and organizational performance.

Now let's focus on the 5 percent of customers lost in the past year. This task will require that you ask some hard questions. First, why did you lose them? You may not like the answers to this question, but without asking, you will keep making the same mistakes with the same results. As any business consultant knows, professional presentations and promises initially bring in customers. But it's a combination of great customer service and timely delivering on promises that brings repeat business and keeps customers loyal. Keep in mind that, according to many business consultants, the lack of customer service accounts for more than 70 percent of customer defections. Having a "keep them sold" plan revised on a regular basis with the account manager will drastically reduce lost clients.

To target your attention on ways to avoid repeating past mistakes, ask yourself:

- What could you have done differently to keep these customers?
- What lessons did you learn from this loss?
- What changes will you implement to prevent future defections to your competition?

These questions aren't about focusing on the past; they're about protecting your future. It costs six times as much in time and company resources to find a new customer compared with keeping an existing customer.

What about the 25 percent of your customer base that currently drives your revenues?

- Who are these customers, and how long have they been with your company?
- How much business do you or your team do with them each year?
- How much personal interaction have you had with them lately?
- In your own customer rankings, where do they fit? Number one? Top three? Top five? Top ten? Or other?

Finally, let's not forget the prospects—potential clients who may hold the key to your organization's financial future. To target your focus on the bottom line, ask yourself these questions about the prospects that make up 70 percent of your potential client base:

- How are you marketing to them?
- What's working? Why? What's not working? Why not?

- How do actual results compare with planned results? If different, why? What's your corrective action? When?

- Is your prospect pipeline full, half-full, or almost empty? What is the recent trend? Which direction is your pipeline of prospects headed? Why? Many times a dwindling pipeline is a symptom of a weak or outdated marketing effort.

- What are you doing about your pipeline trends?

Your ability to retain customers and clients depends on what you do for them. That's why it is critical that you learn to identify the customers that are the biggest (or have the greatest potential to become the biggest) contributors to your organization's bottom-line revenues, and then focus an appropriate amount of your attention on your relationship with those customers.

What are you doing to improve the loyalty of your most valuable customers? Be assured that your competitors are working overtime to make your clients *their* clients. Also remember that your clients will always be more interested in what you can do for them today than in what you have done for them in the past. In today's economy, last month is in the past, and more than six months ago is history. Recent challenges facing your customers, requirements of new laws, regulations, shifting technologies, swings in the business cycle, and nonstop personnel turnover all change the playing field. If you aren't focused on those details every day and responding to them effectively, you and your company run the real risk of becoming irrelevant. If that happens, stand by for a huge new dose of daily tension, anxiety, and stress.

Targeting your focus doesn't have to be a complex process. When was the last time you and your team met with your top customers' key decision makers? These meetings can be relatively short, or even take place over a business lunch. But, you plead, you're *too busy.* Remember your competitors are busy too—but delighted to have lunch any time with your customers. Face-to-face meetings like these help you strengthen your relationship with key customers and remain focused on the issues that are most important to them today. They also create a great opportunity for senior management, colleagues, or key team members to meet with and form a closer, more personal connection with your customers. Senior management and colleagues can thank your important clients for their business and tell them about important strengths you bring to the table. You may be unlikely to discuss your strengths for fear of sounding like a braggart, so let others toot your horn. This is just one suggestion for focusing attention on the clients that are most responsible for adding to your organization's revenues. Whether you make regular phone contact, hold periodic meetings or luncheons, follow up on client events and news releases, or use other methods of focusing attention on your clients, make sure you are allocating that attention wisely. By systematically focusing on critical customers, you send a powerful *we-care-about-you* message that can help retain and grow the loyalty—and potential value—of your most important revenue sources. All clients appreciate that kind of attention. It is your job to make sure you are training that attention where it will do the most good. Remember, all other factors being equal, clients, prospects, and senior management will pick the people they like best to work with them. Always work to be that person.

Step 3: Target Your Decisions/Actions to Have the Greatest Impact on Essential Outcomes

You have seen the value of keeping your most valuable customers squarely in your focus, but what happens when unexpected events result in a drop in revenues? Take a look at this second pie chart. It represents the customer base of a company suffering from just such a situation: revenue is down 50 percent, the new customer pipeline is almost empty, and little new prospect activity is under way. Unfortunately, these setbacks can occur as part of the business cycle. What should *not* occur, however, are these events sneaking up on you. The best way to prevent such ugly surprises is to make sure you spend part of every day focused on factors that most affect your bottom line.

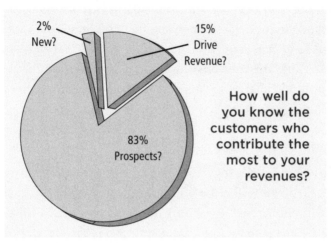

2%
New?

15%
Drive
Revenue?

83%
Prospects?

**How well do
you know the
customers who
contribute the
most to your
revenues?**

Let's use this example to understand what can happen when you don't remain focused on your performance as it relates to the bottom line. As this chart shows, your client revenue sources have dropped from 25 percent to 15 percent. And your annual new customer base has shrunk from 5 percent to 2 percent. Yikes! Your first task is to answer some important questions about that 15 percent group:

- How did your revenue-generating customers drop from 25 to 15 percent? Can you list three factors, in order of importance, that caused this loss? Can your team to do the same thing? Did you have any hunch this drop was coming, or were you blindsided?

- What about the drop from 5 percent to 2 percent of new annual customers? When did you first realize this trend was under way? What action did you take?

- Knowing what you know now, what action should you have taken? How do you plan to avoid or lessen the occurrence of these events in the future?

- What procedures do you plan to implement to provide you and your team with an earlier warning about such potential problems?

- What was the biggest lesson you learned from this experience? What about your team—what did they learn?

I am sure you can think of other questions that can help you focus on and better understand the dynamics of business cycles and how they relate to you, your team, your organization, and its new prospects and customers. If you commit to a comprehensive "keep them sold" plan, you'll lessen the impact of those inevitable negative shifts in the business cycle.

Keeping Your Eyes on the Prize

I have always been highly motivated to share the lessons of my own breakdown in focus with others dealing with tough, stressful situations, because it perfectly illustrates how easy it is for even highly trained people, with carefully drawn plans and a history of relentless preparation, to let their focus wander, just when they need it most. Duke and I knew better. Yet at the most dangerous part of our mission—and we knew this, too—we were not paying attention. My hope is that our experience can help you understand how quickly things can change, morphing a seemingly good situation into a downwardly spiraling disaster.

Like an Olympic athlete, your ability to maintain sharp focus, no matter what, can be the major factor that separates you from your competitors and pushes your performance to its highest levels. By focusing on the right things at the right times, by learning to zero in on the issues that need your immediate attention and target the tasks that have the biggest impact on your bottom line, you take a major step toward mastering this critical element in the Peak Performance Formula. Your goal is to be on the front side of business cycles. Your ability to focus enables you to meet that goal, by making the right decisions as often as possible and, when necessary, by putting the best corrective action in place as soon as possible. The result: you position yourself to take advantage of new opportunities and emerging realities in a changing market—an indispensable task in maintaining peak performance under pressure.

Listening Like a Great Leader

I can't leave this discussion about the role of maintaining focus in achieving peak performance without taking a moment to underscore the importance of paying attention to what goes on around you at work. The advice here is quite simple: give your undivided attention to people you meet and talk with during your workdays. Make them feel important. Listen carefully. Smile. People can feel the warmth of a smile, even on the phone. Listen some more, ask the right questions, listen again, smile some more, and listen.

Have you ever been talking to a good listener on the phone, when a prolonged silence on the other end compels you to ask if they're still there? "I'm still here," they might say. "I'm just listening." Try to become that good listener.

Remember the point in that old business axiom: "Those who talk less, win." When you go into any kind of client or business meeting, turn off your cell phone. You and your company will survive. Be clear with yourself about why you do what you do. Focusing on the people, issues, and ideas around you may not feel like a money-maker, but you can't always assign a dollar value to the gains such focus brings you. For that matter, do you really want money to crowd out everything else within your focus?

Believe me, I have nothing against making money. But I encourage you to remember to pay attention to *everything* that plays a role in your workplace, business, and industry. If you focus solely on making money, you aren't likely to be satisfied. And you certainly aren't assured of success. The ancient Romans observed, "Making money is like drinking salt water—the more you drink, the more you want." Those who drink salt water to quench their thirst ironically die of dehydration. By focusing on the people around you, and the events and issues that matter to them, you position yourself to succeed on multiple levels.

Chapter Debrief

To further explore and understand how the information you've learned in this chapter relates to your peak performance, consider your answers to these questions:

Q } How would you rate your ability to focus on your most important jobs as they emerge during your workday? Would you grade your focus as *good, fair,* or *poor?* Why?

1. When during the day are you best able to focus?

2. Why is your focus better at different times?

3. What are you doing at work during your peak focus times?

4. When do you most frequently find your focus wavering? Why? How do you plan to correct this? When?

5. What factors cause you to lose focus? What can you do to prevent or lessen their occurrence? Have you ever tried to compartmentalize your various tasks and projects?

6. What are you typically doing at work during those unfocused times?

7. What can you do to improve your focus during important work events?

8. How would you rate your daily focus: *good, fair,* or *poor?* Why? What can you do to become better focused?

9. How would you compare your focus: today with your focus this time last year, two years ago, three years ago? What's your trend? Are you getting better, staying the same, or getting worse? Why?

Your response: _____

_____

_____

_____

Q } When evaluating the strength of your relationships with your most important revenue-generating clients, what score do you deserve: *good, fair,* or *poor*? Why? What can you do to improve your score?

1. Do you know which customers, clients, or accounts generate the most revenue for your organization? When was the last time you reviewed this information? Do you have a system in place for periodic revenue and expense reviews of your department? Are you ever surprised at the results? Why, or why not?

2. Do you have a comprehensive "keep them sold" plan in place? Why, or why not? How effective is it?

3. Do you regularly meet with and speak to your critical clients and prospects? Do you have a system in place for regular client contact? How effective is it? How can it be improved? When will you make those improvements?

4. Do you know why new clients chose your organization?

5. Do you know the main reason why you have lost clients or accounts? What corrective actions have you implemented to prevent future client losses?

Your response: _____

_____

_____

_____

Q } In your business interactions, do you spend most of that time talking or listening? Do you ask "good listener" questions?

1. What can you do to become a more effective listener? How would you rate your current listening skills: *good, fair,* or *poor*? Why?

2. How do you think the people who work with and for you rate you as a listener: *good, fair,* or *poor*? Why? How do you plan to improve your listening skills? When will you start?

Your response: _____

_____

_____

_____

CHAPTER FIVE

MEASURING PERFORMANCE

*"Until I have all the facts, I prefer to remain
silent and appear the fool than to open
my mouth and remove any doubt."*

—ABRAHAM LINCOLN

Before every combat mission, the Aces thoroughly analyzed themselves, their teammates, and their enemy in the context of the assigned mission. The Aces were clear on their strengths and weaknesses—what they did well in combat compared with what they did not do well. To be effective, their assessment had to be honest, thorough, pragmatic, performance-based, and tempered by the latest intelligence reports.

The Aces conducted the same assessment of enemy pilots. These assessments determined the Aces' tactical strategy for that day's combat mission, as they sought to pit their strengths against the enemy's weaknesses. Daily intelligence reports allowed the Aces to adjust their mission-planning lens. The Aces knew they had no control over their enemy's actions and, instead, focused attention on what they could control—their own performance. Team performance assessment therefore became a fundamental point of emphasis in all mission briefs. Today, TOPGUN uses that same approach throughout its syllabus.

You too can adopt this method for those important, highly competitive projects at work against well-qualified competitors by continually assessing your performance, along with the latest business and market data. What's working? Why is it successful? What's not working? Why? What needs to change now to operate more effectively? To structure winning business tactics for outperforming your competition, you need to assess their recent performance as well. You want to be able to hit them with your best shot, at the spot where their weaknesses give you the most chance of making an impact.

The Aces knew that in order to maximize your performance (the topic of chapter 6), you first must create a careful and accurate picture of your existing strengths and weaknesses. That's an important lesson for anyone interested in peak performance. No matter how good you are, you can't maintain ongoing success without ongoing improvement. This is a simple but powerful truth that applies to individuals, teams, and organizations.

The National Football League (NFL) provides a good example of just how difficult it can be to gain and maintain an edge in head-to-head competition. All thirty-two NFL teams are directed by the finest head coaches in the sport, many earning between $3 million and $4 million a year. They work as many as fifteen hours a day, seven days a week, for ten months straight. They supervise a staff of some eighteen position coaches (for linebackers, defensive backs, tight-ends, and so on), along with a platoon of trainers, physical therapists, nutritionists, and an extensive medical staff. Each team has the latest multimillion-dollar training facilities. No expense has been spared to produce a winning team. Yet every year, about half the NFL teams lose half or more of their games, and about 30 percent of NFL head coaches are fired. How does that happen with such accomplished coaches and athletes working so long and hard, backed by such a tremendous infrastructure?

TOPGUN taught me the answer to that question: if you aren't constantly working to get better, you stop being good. Aviators selected as TOPGUN students were chosen because of their outstanding airborne performance over time. Like those NFL coaches, these aviators were among the best in their field. But the skill and expertise that got them into TOPGUN wasn't enough to keep them there. Yes, hard work works; every NFL coach and every TOPGUN aviator worked extremely hard to reach that exclusive level. To stay there, however, they had to continually assess and improve their performance, leverage their strengths, and identify and eliminate their weaknesses. Otherwise, they would be asked to leave.

So how can you get better at what you do—and continue to improve, every day? Where do you start? As you will learn in this chapter, you have to begin by determining where you are today. Here we will discuss techniques for assessing your own performance as a decision maker and leader. This chapter also offers ideas for assessing the performance of your team, a fundamental job for any leader who wants to maximize team results and achieve peak performance in his or her own career. We will cap the chapter by taking a closer look at the role of assessment and accountability in monitoring the effectiveness of your strategic plans and tactical activities. By understanding that ongoing assessment is a fundamental step toward ongoing improvement, you will find that you and your team are better prepared to identify and implement the changes necessary to achieve better performance and more winning results.

Gauging Individual Performance

Corporate America has studied the Navy's command screening system for many years. That system is acknowledged in business and military circles as one of the best, nonpolitical, objective promotion systems anywhere in the world. Every six months, fighter squadron commanding officers evaluate their aviators in writing based on how effectively they perform their jobs. These evaluations are called Fitness Reports (Fitreps). Every aviator's performance in specific categories is graded and ranked against his or her peers. Fitreps, like the performance reviews that many businesses conduct on an annual or semiannual schedule, form the basis for who gets promoted, when, and where they are next assigned. Also like a good performance review, all Fitrep debriefs are conducted face-to-face with each aviator and his or her commanding officer (CO). The COs discuss the aviator's performance and answer questions with candor, their feedback aimed at helping the individual take his or her performance to the next level.

During my thirty-year business career, I have been involved in many such performance reviews with subordinates and senior management. Although the Navy's approach may not be directly transferable to your own assessment template, you might consider using some aspects of the Navy's system to assess the individual performance of your direct reports. You can then use this assessment to gain insights into ways that you might work with your staff to help them strengthen their results.

The first step is to gather your facts. The Navy takes this step seriously. When choosing candidates for the job of commanding officer of an aircraft carrier, a selection board composed of three admirals meets for approximately ten days, twelve hours daily, at the Pentagon in Arlington, Virginia. In rooms called "the tank," the board scrutinizes the Fitreps of all candidates. After thorough evaluations of a group of approximately seventy-five candidates, the four best, most-qualified candidates are selected. When assessing the individual performance of your team members, you too should begin by carefully reviewing all previous performance assessments and personnel notes to determine how each individual has progressed during his or her time with your organization, what strengths and weaknesses are recorded in previous reviews, and what progress the individual has made in meeting assigned performance milestones.

Carefully reading previous performance reviews and reviewing personal business plans to determine how the individual has progressed in meeting the goals and performance changes set in those earlier reviews is just the first step in your assessment. After they have assessed previous reviews, the Navy admirals use four criteria to select the best candidates to become commanding officer of a $11.2 billion, 5,500-crew aircraft carrier. You can use these same four fundamental skill sets as performance markers in your own assessments of team members and their qualifications for raises, promotions, and bigger assignments:

1. **Job skills**—The Navy asks the question, "How good is this candidate as an officer and an aviator?" One of your first questions in any assessment should be, "How good is this person at his or her job?" How valuable is he or she to my organization? How effective is he or she as a teammate? Would you rank the person in the top 5 percent of all colleagues? If so, why? If not, what would the individual need to improve in order to rise in the ranking? Make sure you understand clearly why you would rank this candidate's job skills as exceptional, good, average, or weak, and what events or outcomes support that ranking.

2. **Determination**—The Navy terms this criterion the *warrior spirit*, and they gauge it by reviewing the candidate's career-long history of demonstrating a burning desire to engage the enemy in mortal combat. In the workplace, you aren't interested in sending your people into a deadly battle, but you do need to assess their dedication, determination, enthusiasm, and tenacity with all assigned tasks. Pay particular attention to how well they perform under pressure. Again, be thorough and specific in this assessment.

3. **Confidence**—The Navy understands that everyone demonstrates confidence in a different way, but that it is an essential characteristic for consistent winning. When assessing this quality in a team member, ask yourself: Does this individual inspire clients, prospects, senior management, subordinates, and colleagues with confidence? An unshakeable performance-based ability to get the job done creates the kind of self-confidence that radiates trust, respect, and assurance and reflects well on you and your company. Does this individual know his or her job well enough to communicate, by actions,

an unshakable self-confidence? If so, that is genuine confidence, and it rubs off on others.

4. **People skills**—Do others like working with this individual? Measuring people skills from 1 (poor) to 10 (outstanding), the admirals on the Navy's screening board look for 10s. Where does the individual you are assessing fit on your (or your company's) people-skills meter? No matter how technically skilled employees may be, if they can't get along well with colleagues and clients, their effectiveness is limited. Navy admirals often use this metric as a tiebreaker; you might use it in the same way, when ranking the performance of a number of individuals.

Most organizations have standard forms they use to assess individual performance to determine their employees' raises, bonuses, or fitness for promotion. No matter what standardized criteria you use in your individual employee assessments, the four criteria listed here can help you gain valuable insights into any individual's overall level of performance and identify areas where you can work with the individual to help boost that performance to even greater levels. While you're at it, don't forget to give yourself an honest review using the same four criteria you've just read about.

Assessing Your Team's Performance: The Debrief

In today's highly competitive global economy, if you are serious about achieving your work-related goals, you must work smarter. Your career depends on it. You also need your clients to recognize you unquestionably as one of the best in your field. Your career depends on that too. No excuses. But your performance is rarely judged solely on its own merits. As a decision maker or leader, your team's performance plays a major role in how your work is perceived by supervisors, colleagues, clients, and prospects. In spite of shifting markets, economic upheavals, and technological advances, you need to make sure your overall team performance is at its best, in every arena, at all times.

Most MBA programs spend a lot of time talking about managing team performance, but unfortunately, most business classes don't prepare us for what takes place in the real world. Very simply, real-world success at work requires you to not only manage projects but to *lead* people. As with individuals, before you boost team performance, you have to assess your team's strengths and weaknesses. In a volatile business or working environment, those assessments are especially important—and getting the criteria right can be a challenge. Over the past forty years, TOPGUN has had to deal with ever-more-formidable threat levels, unpredictable funding, aging airplanes, and never-ending demands on their time. Sound familiar? And despite all of those challenges, TOPGUN has maintained its place since 1969 as the number-one military aviation training squadron in the world. What does that mean to you? I believe you can adapt the ongoing assessment practices used by the TOPGUN program to improve your own approach to team performance assessment. Here's how those assessments work.

Measuring Situational Awareness

During the ten-week course, students receive approximately forty flights and one hundred dogfights. Each flight and dogfight is thoroughly debriefed by the students and then critiqued by the instructors immediately after the fight. Student situational awareness (SA)—what the students said they *thought* was happening—is compared with what was *really* happening. On almost every occasion, when a student's SA is good, the results are good, and when a student's SA is poor, the results are poor.

All debriefs begin by comparing student prebriefed plans with airborne results. The students meticulously reconstruct each dogfight, including: Who shot whom? When did it happen? How did it happen? Was it a valid shot? Was the shot taken from the observed or unobserved position? What evasive action, if any, did the students under attack take? What happened next? Why? Were the tactics used by their attackers effective? Why did they succeed or fail? The students and instructors also meticulously review the planned versus actual goals for each flight.

As you can see, the TOPGUN data-gathering questions downplay the *who* and focus instead on the *what, how,* and *why.* Even though you won't be debriefing simulated airborne attacks in your performance assessments, you want the information-gathering phase of your assessment process to target what happened in team projects, why it happened, and how each action contributed—positively or negatively—to the outcome. Furthermore, you want to be certain that your team members have a realistic idea of the events involved in their work or projects, so that they (and you) are discussing a single reality rather than multiple misperceptions.

Of course, TOPGUN's experienced instructors knew most of the answers to the questions they asked their students. The instructors are looking for proof that the students know the answers too. While you aren't likely to have TOPGUN's sophisticated tracking data to record your team members' every action, as the decision maker or team leader, you should have a very clear picture of the details surrounding team activities. In other words, *you* must have a strong SA in order to assess your team's SA—and overall performance. Your goal is to be certain that all team members—yourself included—develop clear, tactically correct answers to your questions and, after thorough discussion, a full understanding of the events that marked their performance.

Digging Into the Details: Goods Versus Others

At the conclusion of each debrief, TOPGUN students erase all the flight diagrams on the classroom's whiteboard. On the top left side of the board, they write *Goods*, and on the top right side, *Others*. What the instructors now want to hear from students is their analysis of the goods (actions and decisions that worked well) and others (those that didn't work so well) from this flight. These elements make up the learning points—the assessment takeaways. You can use a similar tactic after you have done your initial review of major workplace events. Remember, your interest at this stage is in gathering your team members' ideas and point of view, not in providing your own assessment.

TOPGUN takes this approach because the instructors want to understand clearly, and they want their students to understand clearly, *why* the students did what they did in the dogfights. With this understanding, they can maximize the training effectiveness of each flight. You can use this same system to bolster the effectiveness of every important interaction for yourself and your colleagues. When everyone understands why they made certain decisions or took specific actions—both goods and others—all of you are in a much better position to improve the team's performance going forward.

One other note: you might choose to divide these performance evaluations into *Good* and *To Be Improved* or some other category names, but the terms you choose here matter. TOPGUN uses the word *others*, instead of the word *bad*, for one simple reason: the instructors don't want students, whose decision making and tactical flying they are trying to influence, listening defensively to the takeaway points. Many educational psychologists tell us that when students begin listening to instruction defensively, their learning capability drops significantly. The same is true of your staff or team. Even if you're right, if your assessment leaves them feeling as though they have been under attack and must defend themselves, your process will lose much of its ability to lay the groundwork for performance improvement. We don't want that at TOPGUN. Nor do you want this in the workplace.

The final step in the TOPGUN process involves the instructors adding their assessment to the debriefing. Up until then, the students have done 90 percent of the talking, with the instructors simply asking questions to prompt more student analysis. Instructors pay strict attention to the accuracy of the students' goods and others. Most students are tough on themselves when assessing their performance in front of this group. However, the instructors are always looking to adjust the students' performance lens for maximum teaching impact. Instructors want the students to make the adjustments and look for the following:

- How are you and your team going to correct today's mistakes?

- What is the most important thing you learned from this flight?

- How are you and your team going to build on this and improve?

You can see the connection this approach has for you and your business. As you review your team's assessment, you need to clarify and refine any areas where you feel the lens needs adjustment. Then you can work with your team on finding ways to improve on *all* events and actions going forward. Think about the deals and projects you and your team have worked on this year— those deals you closed, and those you *almost* closed; projects that achieved your goals, and those that didn't; and those projects

MAKING THE MOST OF YOUR ASSESSMENTS

TOPGUN students, by their very nature, are a resilient, thick-skinned bunch. Every aspect of their performance gets thoroughly assessed every day in a public forum. Although the instructors try to be tactful, the essence of student assessments boils down to student mistakes and expected corrective action. The students get the message loud and clear. They know what has to be corrected and take corrective action. They don't get hung up in any post-assessment doldrums. They move on. You may not have the same luxury with the diverse personalities you deal with at work. So approach your performance assessments tactfully, looking to slowly but steadily improve the way you evaluate performance. (You should realize that you and company policy may sometimes end up in the "others" column. This is good input. Now take corrective action.) And, even at TOPGUN, I always felt strongly that we needed to end most debriefs (assessments) on a positive note by restating one of the biggest goods with a smile. Here's why this is such an important point (which I didn't fully appreciate until later in life).

and deals that didn't come close to meeting your goals, despite all of the effort, time, and company resources you invested in them.

Ask yourself and your team hard questions, such as:

- What did you learn from the deals you closed, the new clients or prospects you landed, or the projects that succeeded in meeting (or even exceeding) goals? Why did they have good results? What did you and your team do to contribute to those results?

- What do you plan to do more effectively the next time with a similar project?

- What could you have done differently with the projects that came close to hitting goals but didn't? What did you learn from those experiences? What changes must you make to convert an almost-successful project into a successful one?

- With the prospects you didn't come close

Because of my speaking business, I'm frequently racing through the world's airports to catch my next flight. About three or four times a year, I run into a former TOPGUN student or instructor whom I flew with or trained years ago. (Many former military aviators are now commercial airline pilots.) We stop for a brief chat. I'm always amazed at what they remember about our short time together. In these unplanned meetings, almost all of my former students take a moment to fondly recall with me the way I taught them something about dogfighting or combat flying. These reminiscences reinforce for me the importance of using the correct style of assessments (debriefs) with your teammates. How you handle these assessments is a critical element of effective leadership and mentoring. American poet Maya Angelou said it best when she reminded us that "people will forget what you said, they'll forget what you did, but people will never forget how you made them feel." Handle your staff assessments the way you would like to be assessed.

to closing or the projects that fell far short of meeting their goals, why did you work on them in the first place?

- What do you plan to do differently the next time?

In answering these questions, you're looking for the same thing that the TOPGUN instructors want from their student debriefs: a rock-solid commitment to take corrective action *now,* to get better. This goods/others technique has been an integral part of TOPGUN's long-term success. You can leverage this same approach to achieve the results you have targeted for yourself, your team, and your organization.

An assessment system of goods and others is easy to implement, and most people love giving their opinions, particularly when asked. It's almost impossible to measure progress without performance debriefs, and you need to have them on an ongoing basis in order for them to form a solid foundation for ongoing improvements. You can adapt the process to work best with your time and team requirements—you might, for example, follow any significant meeting or conference call with short team assessment chats, not lengthy meetings, to assess the goods and the others of the event. Face-to-face debriefs are best. Phone, email, and text messages are not effective ways to conduct goods/others assessments. Your important takeaway here is this: *Any debrief is better than no debrief.* And again, don't forget to give yourself and your team an honest goods/others assessment immediately following key events.

How Are *You* Doing? Taking the Performance Truth Test

Because authentic on-the-job confidence is such an important part of maximizing your peak performance under pressure, it's important that you understand exactly how well you are assessing your own performance. Just as with ongoing team and staff member performance improvement, your ability to continually improve your own performance hinges on your accurate (and ongoing) self-assessment.

If you were to look at your work performance in the mirror, what would you see? Would you like what you see? Why, or why not?

Here is a simple tool to help you paint an accurate picture of your performance as a leader, decision maker, senior manager, and colleague. The five questions below make up your Performance Truth Test. Be honest with yourself as you look in the mirror for your answers; these are great things to keep in mind when you or company policy end up in your teammates' "others" column.

Question 1: Do You Delegate?

It's an old saying, but one that resonates with almost any organizational leader: *There are never enough hours in a day to do everything that has to be done.* But remember this three-word tip on planning: delegate, delegate, delegate. Delegation is a critical skill for decision makers, and one that you need to assess carefully as you work to improve your own performance.

After you have set your daily priorities, as described in chapter 2, you must decide what parts of the A and B projects you *must* do and what parts of those projects you can entrust to others. Before you can be comfortable handing work over, of course, you must have a level of trust in those to whom you're delegating. Do you trust your teammates? Can they get the job done correctly? Is their work timely? Why, or why not? If you have trouble delegating, here are some other questions you should ask yourself about the reasons behind your reluctance:

- What corrective actions must you take to elevate your employee trust meter?
- Have you taken any corrective action in the past? Why, or why not?
- Are you afraid that if they do a good job, they will get the credit and you will not?
- Are you worried that your standing among senior management may diminish?

Perhaps individuals to whom you delegate may not at first perform as well as you. You can delegate authority; you can't delegate responsibility. If teammate performance isn't up to standards after delegating, it's your job to fix it. If you mentor them properly, they could learn to complete many jobs that currently sit on your desk. By pairing mentoring with delegation, you build a deeper bench of qualified staff, even as you free up more of your time so you can focus on the most important tasks that you *must* perform. If your time is worth $300 an hour, why spend it doing a $30-an-hour job? Do the jobs you were hired to do.

Many senior executives don't want to take the risk of a subordinate doing an average job when they can take on the same task and do a great job. That's a valid point, but it depends on the job. Stick to what you were hired to do and let your subordinates do what they were hired to do. If they're not good at it, train them. Mentor them. Then get out of the way and let them do their own job. Still other executives have admitted to me that they are reluctant to delegate because they do not want to risk someone else stealing their thunder. That point isn't valid. If you are serious about reducing your tension, anxiety, and stress, and improving your own work performance, you should become a delegation expert. You may not be correct every time. But the more you delegate, the better you will get at it. Even after delegating, there is still plenty of work for you to do—and plenty of workplace applause for jobs well done.

Question 2: Do You Micromanage?

Micromanaging is a pervasive occupational hazard—one that can sidetrack otherwise top-performing leaders. At some point in our careers, all of us have worked for micromanagers. They want to be involved with everything. Absolutely nothing gets done without their final okay. Working for a micromanager is no fun. Projects move forward, if at all, at a snail's pace. Important decisions are put on hold or postponed. Micromanagers have a difficult time competing against aggressive, well-qualified competitors who don't suffer from the micromanagement bug. Worse yet, subordinates become demoralized, don't learn, and don't improve. Not good!

When you look in the mirror, do you see yourself demanding a thorough review of everything under way in your department? Take a closer look at what you are reviewing now. Are you so indispensable that no one else is qualified to conduct these reviews? Look again in the mirror. Are you overstating your importance? There is a fine line between knowing what is going on in your department and micromanaging. In the end, you have to decide how much attention you must focus on managing the details of every person and task under your watch. Your goal is not to ignore the important details of your team or organization's performance, but to unclutter your days by focusing on the details you *must* attend to. That means learning to delegate wisely.

The further you move up the organizational chain, the more important your ability to delegate becomes. Warren Buffett, one of the richest people in the world and perhaps the most successful investor ever, presides as CEO and chairman of Berkshire Hathaway, Inc., a conglomerate holding company headquartered in Omaha, Nebraska. Berkshire Hathaway owns sixty-three other companies employing 260,000 workers. The companies include GEICO Insurance, Fruit of the Loom, The Pampered Chef, and Dairy Queen. Buffett writes only one letter annually to the CEOs of those companies to give them goals for the year. He never holds meetings or calls them on a regular basis. Few leaders command an empire as large, well constructed, and trained as Warren Buffett's, but the lesson of delegation remains the same for all decision makers: Assign the right people to the right jobs. Stay out of their way, and give them a chance to get it done. Correct as appropriate at the right time.

Question 3: Do You Procrastinate?

Is your work getting done on time? Are the goods or services you promised to customers delivered on schedule? Why, or why not?

Look again in the mirror. Are your habits of procrastination sabotaging your ability to reach peak performance? To assess your tendencies to procrastinate, ask yourself the following questions—and make your answers specific:

- What percent of your company's goods, services, or projects are completed on time? What percent are late? Why? What are you doing about it?

- How do your teammates cope with time-management challenges? Are deadlines realistic? If not, what adjustments are necessary?

- Where are the gaps between production and delivery of your goods or services? Can you shorten or close those gaps? If so, how?

- What new technologies could help you perform more effectively? When are you going to implement them? Why have you not implemented them yet? (Hint: If you reply you are too busy, you need a better, more accurate answer.)

Look in the mirror again. Do you see a micromanager? Or a procrastinator? Or both? Both are usually found together, but your goal is to find neither in your reflection. This is about uncluttering your day to reduce tension, anxiety, and stress at work, and then using your available time to take purposeful action aimed at accomplishing your essential tasks. Those behaviors put you in the best position to maximize your peak performance under pressure every day.

Question 4: Do You Network?

Networking is about more than promoting your career; it's also an essential skill for leaders and decision makers who want to stake a claim in the marketplace and remain aware of the developments and industry shifts shaping that arena. Do you or your teammates go to trade shows, conventions, and industry expos? Trade shows provide an indispensable forum for networking, especially as a sponsor or an exhibitor.

No matter what types of networking activities you participate in, follow-up is critical. According to recent studies, approximately 90 percent of trade-show attendees never make even one follow-up phone call or other contact with those they met at the show. The next 7 percent get in touch with just one attendee, and the remaining 3 percent systematically stayed in touch with five or more of their new networking contacts. Which of these groups do you fall into? What about your team? If you aren't taking advantage of networking opportunities, you aren't pushing your performance as a leader and decision maker to peak levels. Remember that what happens to your career two to three years from now depends on what you do today. Make every networking event count. Establish pre- and post-event prospect follow-up goals, then make sure that you *and* your attending team members are meeting those goals.

Question 5: Are You Accountable?

What does accountability mean to you? For the Aces, it meant doing what they said they were going to do, period. No excuses. If you were to rank the Aces' accountability in an index, they would appear at the top of the rankings. Now look in that mirror one last time. Where do you see your own performance falling on the "accountability index"? Are you doing what you said you would do? The answer is either yes or no. Great promises cleverly presented may win some accolades and appreciation, but timely follow-up action is what impresses people—and keeps them doing business with you.

Whether or not you work directly with customers or clients, you can gain some valuable insights into the importance of accountability by taking a look at your organization's customer service. Strong and responsive customer service is one of the primary ways a company can demonstrate accountability to its marketplace. Recent studies indicate that approximately 75 percent of customer defections are due to poor customer service. Such defections—in customers, clients, accounts, or other important business relationships—are costly. Some surveys have found that it costs six times as much in time and capital to find a new customer compared with servicing and retaining an existing customer.

Now shift your focus to the way you demonstrate accountability in your work. Is your performance congruent with your words? Again, self-discipline is the mortar that holds together the essential elements of your peak performance, and nowhere is your self-discipline more evident than in the way you manage and demonstrate accountability.

As a decision maker, accountability starts with you. Are you holding yourself responsible for your actions? Do you hold others on your staff or team accountable for their actions? Is everybody clear about what is expected of them? What happens if products or services are not delivered on time? Does everyone understand the consequences for missed actions or deadlines? Consequences in your organization for such lapses don't have to be harsh, but you must clearly define and enforce them. Your most effective tool for promoting accountability, however, and for maximizing your own performance, is your own good example. Make your accountability strong, constant, and transparent for everyone to see. Remember how much we dislike the hypocrisy of do-as-I-say-not-what-I-do behavior. By holding yourself accountable for meeting your commitments and for assessing your accountability on an ongoing basis, you are in a better position to set the kind of example you want your team to follow. And, in the process, you will be working to drive your performance as a decision maker, leader, and teammate to ever-higher levels.

Monitoring Effectiveness

As you have just seen, accountability is a major factor in our personal, professional, and organizational performance. But the assessment techniques you have learned about in this chapter are all about monitoring *effectiveness.* When you assess your performance—both your own and that of your team or organization—you are, in essence, monitoring the effectiveness of everything you do.

YOUR OWN DAILY GOODS AND OTHERS ASSESSMENT

Here is the most important thing you can do to use ongoing assessment as a key to ongoing improvement: Take a few minutes at the end of your workday, with that day's daily action plan in front of you, to assess your performance. Compare what you had planned with what you accomplished. How did you do? What are your goods and others? (Doesn't it feel great to check things off your list as done?) Like the Aces, you can remain at the top of your game by consistently reviewing how well you performed today and by asking yourself tough questions about how you can be better tomorrow and every day that follows. Without its rigorous self-assessment system, TOPGUN would have gone out of business years ago. Without some regular and frequent self-assessment system in place, improved performance occurs more by chance than by design, and you will never lead yourself, your team, or your company to higher performance levels.

The benefits of accountability have been with us long before the TOPGUN program began or the first Ace won his title. Centuries ago, the ancient Romans constructed some 2,000 bridges in Italy. Today, most are still standing and operational. Roman bridges feature semicircle arches. They were made by laborers standing on wooden scaffolding as they laid the stones and poured the cement. When each bridge was finished and the scaffolding removed, a ceremony followed to test the structure. The architect, the project engineer, and the head contractor all stood under the bridge while an entire Roman legion of some 1,500 troops with their horses, chariots, and full battle equipment marched across in formation. It was a field test. The folks who had built the bridge were required to put their lives at risk to show their work was solid. This extreme example of accountability was also a very useful technique for monitoring the effectiveness of Rome's construction technologies and practices. Rome wasn't built in a day, but it was well built *every* day. History has no record of even one Roman bridge collapsing while undergoing the "legion test."

Monitoring effectiveness is at the heart of TOPGUN's commitment to performance excellence. All of TOPGUN's strategic, operational, and tactical decisions are facts-based. When TOPGUN instructors teach combat tactics, they rely on current, airborne-verified data. What tactics will likely work against today's threats? Why? What are the backup tactics? What is not working in training today? Can it be fixed quickly? How? What are the strengths and weaknesses of our planes? Of our enemy's planes? These assessments enable TOPGUN instructors to notice immediately when their tactics and equipment are no longer effective.

When Navy and Marine aircrews fly over enemy territory, TOPGUN instructors are held accountable for the training and readiness of those crew members. No excuses. When any lapses occur or results are less than expected, TOPGUN instructors scrutinize class assessments, flight debriefs, and the latest intelligence reports. Then they meet to quickly adjust their tactics. The goal is simple: they want to promptly and professionally regain effectiveness against new and emerging threats. What about you, your team, and your company? How are you monitoring the effectiveness of what you do? When your results aren't going as planned or when a procedure, product, or team member is no longer effective, what do you do? Are you holding yourself accountable for corrective action? Or are you looking the other way, too busy being busy or ignoring the problem altogether? Certain problems, left unchecked, can have a devastating effect on your team and organization's performance. Remember: good team accountability starts with you. Set a good example. Then demand that all others on your team be held accountable for their performance. When you are monitoring the effectiveness of your team or organization, remember that your assessment process is an important source for soliciting the input of others.

TOPGUN analyzes and debates all sides thoroughly before deciding what tactics to teach, modify, or eliminate. The TOPGUN commanding officer, who holds 51 percent of the vote, recognizes the benefit of soliciting input first. Many psychologists agree that when most people have an opportunity to offer input right from the beginning, they are more likely to accept the decisions. In the next chapter, we discuss the important work of maximizing performance, which in most cases involves adopting new rules, models, or other changes. Before we move on to that discussion, let's take a minute to overview the basic steps of using assessment data as an accurate indicator and springboard for performance improvement.

Analyzing the Facts

Those syllabus decisions made by TOPGUN instructors, with feedback from each graduating class, all had one critical ingredient: gathering the facts necessary to make those decisions. When we act on incomplete or faulty information, we aren't going to make the strongest decisions or achieve the strongest results.

There is an interesting story about a young student whose father was called in by the headmaster to meet about the student's poor performance. The headmaster and teacher explained that this student paid no attention in class and was, by all appearances, not very intelligent. The story goes that the school strongly recommended that the student be enrolled in a vocational school, where he stood a better chance of finishing and finding a job in a useful trade. When the father asked the headmaster and teacher if they had tested his son or quizzed him in class to be certain that he wasn't absorbing information, they admitted that they hadn't. They had based their opinion strictly on the teacher's observation and on the young student's lack of class participation. The father asked the teacher and headmaster to give his son some more time, call on him in class, and see how he did when he was tested. Do you know the identity of this young, seemingly not very bright student? Albert Einstein—a name that today is synonymous with genius.

The teacher and headmaster should have done their homework before they hauled Albert Einstein's father in to tell him his son wasn't able to cut it in school. They jumped to the wrong conclusion because they did not take the time to get the facts. Has this ever happened to you? Think how wrong these two were when you consider the potential impact that incomplete or erroneous information can have on your strategic, operational, and tactical decisions. Also consider the effect on your business when competitors aren't making the same mistakes and have more complete and accurate information than you have. Guess who wins the new clients and closes the most and best deals?

Do your homework and, to position yourself for peak performance under pressure, complete your research and analysis. Look into all the pertinent facts, including a thorough review of the goods and others. Check them for validity before making important decisions.

Acting on Your Analysis

Avoid falling into the trap of analysis paralysis. Once you have completed your due diligence, take appropriate action. The final critical step in achieving peak performance is implementing all those good ideas. Here we can look to Albert Einstein for another valuable lesson.

In his later life, when Einstein enjoyed worldwide recognition as a brilliant physicist, he was asked by a reporter if he considered himself the smartest man in the world. Einstein smiled and answered no. He told the reporter that others in his group were just as smart. What set him apart, Einstein said, was that he cared more about his work than the others. Acting on your analysis of ongoing assessments is how you show that you care about your performance, your team's performance, and your company's or organization's success.

Consider these questions:

- What makes you different from your competitors?
- Do you care about your work more than your competitors do? How do you know?
- If so, is it obvious to your clients?

- If not, then how do you plan to show them? With actions or words?
- Are you credible with your clients? Why, or why not?
- What is your competitive advantage?
- Why is it unique to you?

Again, to maximize your peak performance under pressure, you must have carefully planned answers to these questions. Your answers will change over time. Does that mean you will need to change the way you do things? Definitely. The lesson we learned from TOPGUN is that by taking the approach of goods/others in systematic reviews, you use an excellent battle-tested system to adjust, refine, and further improve what you do while making yourself and your teammates better.

I started my association with Naval Fighter Aviation in the late 1960s. Despite the many changes in planes, missiles, and tactics that have taken place since then, I've noticed that the qualities of the best fighter pilots have remained the same. They never sat in the debriefs satisfied with themselves. They were aware of what they didn't know and had a fanatical passion to improve their effectiveness. They told themselves that although they were great up there today, they were going to be greater up there tomorrow. Through your ongoing assessment and analysis, you can continually track the effectiveness of your performance. And that's how you build the foundation of continuous improvement that underlies any peak performance. As the Aces could tell you, "The day you stop wanting to be better is the day you stop being good."

Chapter Debrief

To further explore and understand how the information you've learned in this chapter relates to your peak performance, consider your answers to these questions:

Q } Do you have a system in place to assess the effectiveness of your performance at the end of each workday?

1. What's the trend with your daily performance based on your assessments: *getting better, staying the same,* or *getting weaker*?

2. Are you achieving your stated goals? Are you even close? Why, or why not?

3. Are you closing the right deals?

4. Is your work done on time?

5. How effectively are you closing deals and completing projects?

6. Are you working on the right deals and projects? How do you know?

Your response: _____

_____

_____

_____

Q } How do you feel when tough problems suddenly pop up during your workday? How would you rate your ability to handle obstacles: *good, fair,* or *poor*?

1. What are the toughest obstacles you face today? How are you dealing with them?

2. Are they different from last year's toughest obstacles?

3. What steps can you take to improve your ability to handle tough new problems at work?

4. What resources do you need to more effectively handle these challenges?

Your response: _____

_____

_____

_____

Q } As unexpected events of your workday unfold, do you have a good grasp of their relevance to your bottom line? What actions or adjustments do you then implement? How do you measure the effectiveness of these actions and adjustments?

1. How is your situational awareness on the job?

2. How can you make your SA better?

3. In dealing with clients, competitors, senior management, subordinates, and colleagues, are you able to distinguish between the surface reasons and the real reasons for their actions?

Your response: _____

_____

_____

_____

Q } Do you have a system in place for holding yourself accountable to your teammates and senior management? Is your accountability strategy transparent for all to see? Why, or why not?

1. How do you demonstrate strong accountability in your workplace? Is it transparent?

2. How do you deal with lapses in accountability among your team members?

3. How can you use assessment to monitor the effectiveness of your work? Of your team's work? Of your organization's overall efforts to fulfill its mission and meet its goals?

Your response: _____

_____

_____

_____

CHAPTER SIX

MAXIMIZING PERFORMANCE

"Our greatest glory is not in never failing,
but in rising every time we fall."
—CONFUCIUS

If you have ever seen photos or videos of a U.S. Navy aircraft carrier conducting flight operations, you have had a glimpse of a truly remarkable event. Exactly forty-five minutes before scheduled takeoff, naval aviators—most in their late twenties and eager for the challenges ahead—strap into twenty tactical jet aircraft spotted within feet of each other along the flight deck. On cue, the pilots flip a switch and fire up their engines. The quiet is suddenly shattered by a low-groaning whine that quickly turns into an ear-splitting, high-pitched roar as jet engines scream to life. Then four jets at a time taxi up for launch. With their afterburners spitting orange flames, the thirty-ton jets launch off the ship in a slingshot-like blast from steam-powered catapults, reaching speeds of 160 mph in just seconds. Within ten minutes, all twenty jets are airborne.

A quick re-shuffle has the flight deck reconfigured to land twenty jets from the previous launch. The ship is traveling at 20 mph, pitching and rolling with the sea, its landing area just 120 feet long and 20 feet wide.

To the Navy pilots who approach this floating runway every night, the carrier—a city of steel about 1,100 feet long and 250 feet wide with a crew of 5,500 sailors—can look like a postage stamp bobbing in a vast ocean.

The jets alternate landing at one-minute intervals, their tail-hooks mounted below the engines, ready to catch a thick arresting cable fastened across the deck. As each jet's arresting hook hits the steel flight deck, a cascade of sparks fly from the metal-on-metal grind of the 130 mph landing and an ear-splitting roar erupts as the jet screeches to a halt. The pilot taxis out of the arresting cable, just as another jet is on final approach, seconds from touchdown. During the twelve hours of flight operations, this twenty-plane launch-recover cycle repeats seven times. The landings are precise and dangerous work, conducted by a highly trained and motivated crew under the expert leadership of the ship's commanding officer, the captain.

Carriers demand strong leadership skills from their captains and precision performance throughout the chain of command. As I mentioned earlier, during flight operations, crew members work eighteen-hour days, seven days a week, and many earn less than the minimum wage. Every month, some 250 sailors, many of them raw recruits, report in to replace an equal number who are rotating out. The ship has a completely new crew every thirty months, almost 90 percent of them under age twenty-two. The tempo of flight operations is always high-speed and dangerous. Any crew mistakes, particularly on the flight deck, could cause major injury or death. I can't think of a better illustration of teams consistently attaining peak performance under pressure—or a better example of the essential need for the kind of maximized performance that results from ongoing improvement.

In the many years I've spent working with top military and business leaders, I've seen that ambition, drive, and hard work aren't enough to guarantee peak performance, especially in the face of unrelenting workplace pressure. Yes, those qualities will help you accomplish some of your goals and achieve some level of success. But if you want to maximize your results in *any* high-pressure environment, you also need to continually work to improve your performance and that of your team and organization.

This chapter is all about achieving more. Here you learn a number of far-ranging techniques for attaching your ambition and hard work to the driving engine of ever-higher goals and standards. To help you in that work, this chapter offers a number of ideas for building unshakeable self-discipline and confidence. You also learn techniques for sharpening your skills in interacting with and influencing those around you, including clients, colleagues, team members, and supervisors. We will take a closer look at specific ideas for maximizing the essential habits and skills of leadership—the confidence, discipline, and empathy that drive your ability to put yourself in the place of the people you lead, to understand their motivations and challenges, and to fully acknowledge and credit them for their contributions. We also will talk about some specific ways you can help instill some of these same skills in your team members. Then they will feel the same drive to continually raise their own levels of performance, even in the fast and furious environment of relentless competition and rapidly shifting global markets.

Together, the tools and techniques you learn here will help you *and* your team or organization achieve the kind of ongoing improvement that answers the challenge of a truth you read very early in this book: *The moment you stop wanting to get better is the moment you stop being good.*

Becoming a More Effective Leader

How does the captain of a Navy aircraft carrier motivate his crew to work such long hours for so little pay and direct the almost continuous training involved in managing an ever-changing crew complement? How does the captain keep these young sailors pumped up about their work over a ten-month deployment? The answers to these questions all lie in the mastery of habits and skills that often

142

are overlooked in the discussion of leadership. Let's examine some methods behind that mastery.

Developing the Three Fundamental Habits of Strong Leadership

There are many examples of exceptional leadership that during chaotic times influenced the course of history. Here I want to offer three such examples, each of which illustrates one of the three essential habits demonstrated by strong, effective leaders everywhere:

1. Caring about your team's challenges and perspectives

2. Leading by example

3. Giving your team the credit it deserves

For the first of these examples, let's look back to the leadership of Abraham Lincoln. Despite overwhelming odds, Lincoln won the 1860 presidential race and led his country during the Civil War, the most divisive time in the history of the Republic. Pulitzer Prize–winning author Doris Kearns Goodwin notes in her book

DIFFERENTIATING LEADERSHIP FROM MANAGEMENT

As I travel around the country, speaking at business conventions and interviewing senior executives in all types of industries, I hear a lot about management techniques. This focus totally misses the point of true leadership. All military officers learn, right from the beginning of their careers, that you *manage* programs, but you *lead* people. As former Chairman of the Joint Chiefs General Colin Powell once said: "Leadership is the art of doing more than the science of management says is possible."

As you have seen, those nuclear-powered aircraft carrier captains *must* have exceptional people skills. Yes, they are also bright. All graduated at or near the top of their class in physics or engineering and have advanced degrees in physics or engineering from leading universities. Their critical education, however, continued long after they graduated, as they learned how to understand and deal effectively with the people they work with—and for. To these captains, and for all leaders who want to maximize their performance, well-developed people skills are essential elements in their toolkit for the job of leadership.

Team of Rivals that President Lincoln's commitment to understanding the perspectives and appreciating the concerns and challenges of those he worked with were fundamental elements of the brilliant leadership he displayed during those tumultuous times. "Lincoln's success was the result of character that had been forged by experiences that raised him above his more privileged and accomplished rivals," Kearns Goodwin writes. "He won because he possessed an extraordinary ability to put himself in the place of other men, to experience what they were feeling, to understand their motives and desires." Those words carry an important lesson in leadership for all of us.

Do you take the time at work to put yourself in the place of others? Do you think about what your people feel about the projects, challenges, and deadlines they face every day? Do you have any understanding of their motives and desires—which are the sources of what they say and do each day at work? If you deflect such questions by saying you are too busy or don't have the time, remember this: President Lincoln was busy too. If he found time for this kind of analysis, we all should be able to do the same.

The military provides our next example of an essential element of leadership, a compelling story that involves a little-known Army sergeant-of-the-guard at Arlington National Cemetery's Tomb of the Unknowns. The white marble vault of the Tomb of the Unknowns rests in an open public square on a hill overlooking the Potomac River and Washington, DC. It contains graves holding the remains of unidentified soldiers killed in battles during America's armed conflicts. Since 1931, honor guards have stood watch at the Tomb, twenty-four hours a day, seven days a week, even in the stormiest of times.

In 2003, Isabel, a category 4 hurricane, was forecasted to slam into Washington, DC, with winds of more than 100 mph and torrential rains. The hurricane roared up the Eastern Seaboard, leaving destruction in its wake. In preparation, officials in the Washington area closed government offices, canceled schools, and shut businesses for two days. Several hours before the hurricane's expected arrival, a government official called the officer-in-charge at the Tomb, informing him of the hurricane's forecasted danger. For the first time in the history of the Tomb, guards were given the option to withdraw to safer positions if necessary. It would be up to this sergeant to decide when and if to withdraw the guards to a safer place. The officer and his sergeant-of-the-guard drew up a contingency plan for allowing sentinels to seek shelter under the Tomb's arches or inside its trophy room if conditions became perilous.

Indeed, Hurricane Isabel turned out to be even more severe than predicted. Winds exceeded 125 mph, and driving rains bucketed down, drenching the area over seven hours. The hurricane felled twenty-four mature trees in Arlington National Cemetery, including two near the Tomb. When media reporters later inquired about the status of the watch, they learned that the sergeant decided not to have his sentinels seek shelter. They also learned that the sergeant stood almost all the watches himself, explaining that in light of the sacrifices being made by his numerous friends and comrades fighting in Iraq and Afghanistan, he refused to let "a little wind and rain" drive him from his duty to remain on watch. He and others in his unit felt they were honoring the troops who had come before them.

That sergeant was out in front, leading by example, and thereby demonstrating one of the most important qualities of effective leaders. He had already thought through the likely what-if scenarios. He had an exit strategy in place in case this already hazardous situation worsened. Then he made a tough decision and led the way in following through with it. The leadership lesson he so bravely illustrated? *He didn't ask his people to do something he wasn't willing to do first.*

Our final leadership lesson involves another venerable national monument, the Vietnam Veterans Memorial in Washington, DC, and another military leader, General Peter Pace. General Pace is a former Chairman of the Joint Chiefs of Staff, a unique military group composed of the leaders of the Army, Navy, Air Force, and Marine Corps that serves as the principal military advisor to the president, the National Security Council, and the Secretary of Defense. In September 2007, General Pace retired after forty years of service, which included time in Vietnam, where he was a Rifle Company Commander before rising through the ranks to become the first Marine selected as the Chairman of the Joint Chiefs of Staff.

The Vietnam Memorial has two adjoining dark stone walls about 250 feet long, engraved with the names of 58,267 U.S. Armed Forces men and women who died during that war. Veterans simply call it The Wall. It provides them the chance to "visit" old comrades and friends. A friend of mine visiting The Wall in early October 2007 noticed a tall, distinguished civilian standing by it. My friend thought the civilian bore a remarkable resemblance to General Pace, but he quickly dismissed the idea because he thought the general was still in the service, and this man was out of uniform.

After some minutes, the man left. Out of curiosity, my friend went over to the section where this tall civilian had been standing. He saw that three cards were propped against that section. When he stepped closer to read them, he was stunned by what he saw. Pinned to the bottom of one card was a row of four stars, from the shoulder of the General's uniform jacket. My friend read the handwritten message: "For Guido Farinaro, USMC. These are yours—not mine! With love and respect, your platoon leader, Pete Pace."

With this remarkable act, General Pace demonstrated just one example of his commitment to honoring the contributions—and sacrifices—of those under his leadership. The general, like other leaders who have risen to the top of their profession, offers us a powerful lesson in this simple truth: *It's amazing what you can accomplish when you don't mind who gets the credit.*

Would *you* go into combat with or for these leaders? More appropriately, are your people willing to follow your leadership into even the most demanding daily work-related "combat"? Three stories, three illustrations of the three essential elements of strong leadership. Ask yourself:

- Do you demonstrate that you care about your team?
- Are you consistently willing to lead by example?
- Are you quick to acknowledge the contributions of others?

If you can incorporate these three basic leadership principles into your daily routine at work, the effectiveness of your leadership will skyrocket, regardless of the tough pressures you face every day at work. You also will earn the respect of all who come into contact with you.

Developing Your Ability to Interact and Influence

How does TOPGUN most effectively get its points across to a wide variety of student personality types? The way their teaching points are presented may register clearly with one student but hardly make an impression on another. As a leader, your ability to present your ideas clearly and effectively to the diverse group of people you must try to influence every day is an important factor in maximizing your performance. At TOPGUN, we are aware that our students, like your people in business, are all wired differently. We are very diligent—as you should be—in personalizing our message, one student at a time, for maximum learning. That means thinking about your listeners as well as your ideas. To communicate most effectively, mentally tick through your points ahead of time and take a moment to determine how to best target those ideas toward your listener. Your goal is to present your information in a way that best suits the personality type of the person you are trying to influence. As a staff, TOPGUN instructors constantly discuss student performance. We are keenly interested in how to best present teaching points for each individual's maximum learning. And we try to follow the general rule of praising in public and criticizing in private.

If you are serious about influencing your people in a manner consistent with your way of thinking, bear in mind that it is all about *them*. When you talk to your people, listen, pay attention, ask relevant questions. Listen some more. Learn from *them*! Then package your message and instructions around the benefits to *them* in a manner that best suits *them*. That's what TOPGUN does, and we've been getting awesome results every year throughout the history of the program.

Sure, you may plead that you are too busy to spend that amount of time in preparing to talk with a customer or colleague. But this is about being productive. To remain productive, even when the going gets tough, you have to be able to get the right things done with the right people at the right time. This is what maximizing your peak performance under pressure is all about. If your style is to launch spur-of-the-moment instructions to your staff, bear in mind that many of those directives run the risk of being ignored. When people have too much unfiltered information coming at them from different directions, they often treat it with selective neglect. That can lead to inaction. Then promising sources for increased revenue or new business may be overlooked.

When this happens, subordinates and senior management alike can become frustrated, upset, and sometimes angry. This can lead to harsh words that cause hard feelings and result in a cascade of frustrating situations, escalating pressures, and personality conflicts. Those negatives will work against all of your other efforts to maximize your performance and results. You have to align the thinking, goals, and priorities of everyone involved in a project with those of the overall team or organization, to keep everyone moving purposefully toward the same targeted outcomes. That means you have to perfect your skills at interacting with and influencing the people you work with every day—clients, prospects, senior management, subordinates, and vendors.

How you handle yourself in such interactions with your people will influence the outcome. Why take the chance of missing the mark? In today's business world, there is little margin for error. So invest the time and think about how the people on the other end of your interactions like to get started. Remember, there are many approaches to presenting the same information to different people. Are they analytical? Visually oriented? Artistic right-brain types, straight-forward left-brainers, or some combination of the two? Do they want a slant that emphasizes engineering, marketing, sales, or finances? They won't tell you. You'll have to figure that out on your own.

Learning From the Superstars

How do you become that shrewd executive or respected decision maker? Do what the Aces did, and get to know the superstars in your company and industry. Look for mentors—well-respected professionals with a record of success. You find them at company conventions, regional meetings, all-hands training sessions, and trade shows. Offer to buy them lunch or a drink after the scheduled meetings. Interview them to find out how they succeeded. Most are happy to tell you their story, if you simply ask.

The right mentors are a terrific source of knowledge, wisdom, and lessons learned. Aces, like all top decision makers, are

MEET MR. CARNEGIE

So how do you improve your people skills? Dale Carnegie's book *How to Win Friends and Influence People* has terrific advice on this topic. Although the book was first published seventy-five years ago, its core message has as much relevance and value today as it did when the book first hit the shelves. Today, worldwide sales of *How to Win Friends and Influence People* top 15 million copies. You've heard that expression "If you want to learn something new, read an old book." Check this one out. You'll be glad you did, and your people skills will soar.

made, not born. All started as inexperienced rookies. Aces worked smart and incredibly hard, and they all found mentors. As a young aviator, I spent countless hours talking with experienced combat veterans, TOPGUN instructors, and Aces. My goal was to learn how they got to where I wanted to go. Those discussions proved to be an invaluable tool for learning. They hastened my development, and I made lifelong friends in the process. The knowledge these mentors shared with me also played a key role in my later success in combat and business.

Will your pride be hurt by these sessions? Who cares? Look at what you receive in return. You get excellent new industry contacts and gain greater insight into how your industry superstars work. You'll learn how to better rank team projects according to importance, how to complete tough assignments more quickly, and how to approach the kinds of decisions that keep you and your team on track and performing at your best despite the many escalating pressures at work.

Mentors can help you grow throughout your career. If you are working to become a top sales leader, for example, don't forget to ask for your mentor's best techniques for qualifying prospects, retaining long-standing customers, and finding new business.

When I started my career as a commercial real estate salesman with Coldwell Banker, the company had a sales force of more than 12,000. In my first year there, the top salesperson was Jerry Cole. His office was about an hour's drive away. I called and asked to meet him at a convenient time. I wanted to learn what he did to take the company's lead sales position. At our meeting, he patiently answered all my questions and offered great advice from lessons he had learned on his way to the top. I came away with a wealth of ideas and a clear list of objectives. I later enjoyed the same kind of conversations with the company's top sales professional in my region and the top producer in the eastern United States. The great advice and guidance of these top performers accelerated my professional development and laid out a clear path toward where I wanted to go.

I still remember the generosity of every one of my mentors. When young executives and fighter pilots contact me for the same purpose, I am happy to return the favor. In today's workplace, one lesson our moms taught us when we were growing up still applies: *What goes around comes around.* To maximize your leadership skills and workplace performance, find a good mentor—and *be* a good mentor.

Checking in on Your Client Credibility

The last student flight at TOPGUN is the final exam, called the "Class Graduation Strike." Ten student jets compete as friendlies against twelve to fifteen TOPGUN jets flying as enemies. The students are highly motivated to win. They'll remember the outcome of their last flight at TOPGUN for the rest of their lives. Their instructors are just as determined to win. It's an intense flight, performed with great skill, professionalism, and precision. Most of the time, the students have learned their

TAKING TIME TO REFOCUS BEFORE IMPORTANT INTERACTIONS

I recommend that, before you begin your next important presentation, meeting, or other business interaction event, you take a moment to slow down, breathe deeply, and do a quick refresh on the following "what" questions about the people you will meet:

- What is most important to them?
- What is the benefit of your product or services to them? What is the biggest benefit?
- What are their likely concerns— and their biggest concerns?
- What can you offer to reduce or eliminate those concerns?
- What questions can you expect from them, and what are your best answers?
- What can you offer that sets you, your product or service, and your company apart from your competitors?
- What do you want to accomplish with this event? What's your takeaway goal?

Of course, everyone has his or her own preferences when it comes to interaction. Some like small talk first, discussing sports, family, or other general topics. Others want to get right to the point, and often, that means telling you about their problems with a project or deal you are trying to complete. The onus is on you to know ahead of time some likely conversation starters for the individuals you will be interacting with. All top salespeople know that this kind of warm-up is critical. These top salespeople think ahead of time about the best way of interacting with their clients, based on their knowledge of them and the purpose of the meeting. That's smart business. Many of your interactions at work and in life are nothing more than sales situations. If you approach these interactions with forethought, you increase your chances of winning; if you don't, you increase your chances of losing. Why risk unnecessary loss in today's performance-based workplace?

lessons well and perform with distinction.

After this final flight's debrief, one of the most important parts of the course takes place for the instructors. The graduating class of eighteen to twenty students convenes in the academic classroom with all thirty-one instructors for what is called the "Class Debrief." You've read about debriefs frequently in this book; this final one functions as the report card for TOPGUN. All instructors sit with pens and legal pads, listen, and take notes, as the students offer their assessment of the effectiveness of the entire TOPGUN course. Instructors are there for one reason: to listen and learn. They offer no explanations, comments, or rebuttals. The goods and others of the syllabus, as seen through the eyes of their customers—the students—are the instructors' primary interest. TOPGUN takes these debriefs very seriously. They present a unique opportunity to get direct performance feedback.

Think about what a bonanza of information you could get from your clients if you sat down with them periodically to gather their assessment of the strengths and weaknesses—the goods and others—of your performance. Do you take time to gather, carefully review, and act upon customer or client feedback? I have seen that many leaders and decision makers are too busy working on the next project, the next deal, a mushrooming crisis, or deadlines to give much additional thought to the work they just completed. TOPGUN instructors are under the same pressure to keep moving forward. They also are always on the go. True, their work doesn't have money at risk or substantial fees on the table. They deal with a more personal risk—their lives and those of their students. As a matter of survival, they need to adjust, change when necessary, and get better. Like the Aces, if you want to continually raise the bar on your personal and organizational performance, you have to learn to seek—and use—client feedback. Not only your success, but your *survival* at work depends on it.

RUNNING EFFECTIVE MEETINGS

According to a recently published study of 1,000 employees by Opinion Matters, a London-based market research firm, office workers spend a minimum of four hours a week in meetings and regard more than half of them as a waste of time. A recent study by Salary.com revealed that 47 percent of 3,164 employees interviewed identified meetings as the biggest time-waster in their office. So, as the leader of your team, are you running good meetings? What are you doing to make your meetings productive and effective? Most importantly, what can you do to get the maximum results from the meetings you lead and attend?

To help you answer those questions, here are some techniques for getting the most from meetings. I have seen these tactics used successfully at TOPGUN and in the hundreds of business meetings I've attended as a professional speaker:

- Try to schedule your meetings in the morning—the earlier the better. I try *never* to schedule meetings immediately after lunch or in the late afternoon or evening. The best days for meetings are Tuesday, Wednesday, and Thursday.

Here is how TOPGUN uses these customer-performance evaluations to get better. The day after the class graduation, a Saturday, all thirty-one instructors return to the same room for a meeting on the Class Debrief. This meeting is called a Staffex, and it starts promptly at 8:00 a.m. The instructors painstakingly scrutinize everything about their performance, particularly the goods and others identified by the just-graduated class. The instructors also thoroughly debate important syllabus questions, with a keen eye toward what areas of instruction need less or more emphasis, what's missing, unnecessary, or needs a new approach.

When the topic turns to the areas of instruction that appear to be going well, the discussion always intensifies. These instructors are very sensitive to the notion that without change, there is no progress. They know they can't provide their students with the best, most up-to-date training if, for example, they present the same information year after year. These meetings

- Take the time to adequately prepare yourself at least one or two days before the meeting. I can't tell you how many times I have observed poorly prepared senior executives or team leaders bumbling through a weak set of discussion points while the attendees sit there with that glazed-donut look, bored to tears.

- Have a written agenda with a list of scheduled speakers, discussion points, and time allocated for each point. Send it out well in advance to all attendees—and follow it. Plan ahead for coffee, snacks, or other food that you will need delivered to the room. Build breaks into your agenda as appropriate (at least every fifty minutes) to give attendees time to use the restroom and check messages, and to help keep them alert and focused.

- Get to the meeting site at least thirty minutes before it begins. Check out the room, seating, lighting, and any equipment you will use. Clear away any cups or other litter left by previous users, and clear any notes left on the whiteboard or flip chart. Turn the thermostat down to at least 68 degrees.

(Continued on page 154)

154

aren't rushed. At the end, all instructors must be satisfied that the right syllabus decisions are reached and that they have pinpointed the right items for action with clearly defined completion dates.

Don't think for a moment that the TOPGUN instructors who attend those Staffex meetings are one big, happy family, because they aren't. TOPGUN has a diverse collection of personalities all chomping at the bit to share their wisdom. Just like your team or organization, there are many different, strong opinions on what should be changed and how to proceed. But the instructors never stop working to ensure that they are teaching the latest tactics to defeat more, better, increasingly sophisticated new threats. They are highly motivated to improve the TOPGUN syllabus and maximize their skill in presenting it. They know that in today's uncertain world, if they stay the same, they will fall behind. That's a surefire recipe for disaster.

For any business, making a change for the sake of change

(Continued from page 153)

- Check your appearance, look sharp, and be the first to arrive for the meeting. Then relax. Sure, messages are piling up and you have a zillion return calls to make, but those can wait until later. Right now, you don't need to be distracted by them.

- Greet the attendees as they arrive. This is pre-meeting warm-up time. Use it to have a word or two with as many attendees as possible.

- Let all attendees know that it's your policy to start and end every meeting exactly on time; then follow your policy (unless you can end the meeting before the scheduled time, which will earn you special thanks from all attendees). If you can't see a clock from your position in the room, lay your watch where you can see it before you begin speaking.

- Ask everyone at the meeting to turn off all cell phones and portable devices. I've been in meetings in which more than half of the attendees are checking email or texting. These folks are oblivious to any information being presented in the meeting—and they can distract those around them who are trying to listen.

- Be prepared to deal with know-it-alls and negativity champions among your attendees. Don't get flustered or angry, and don't let them take over your meeting. If necessary, thank speakers who go over the allotted time and tell them you're happy to discuss their points further after the meeting. Then move on.

- Expect long-winded discussion on certain topics. Do your what-if preparation in advance and have your responses ready. You're not running a prolonged debate, so avoid that trap. You want the tricky issues on the table for discussion, but always keep a sharp eye on moving forward with potential solutions. Stay on your timeline.

The art of running good meetings is your responsibility. It's also part of your job as a leader. Running good meetings is a skill that can be learned and perfected over time if you're serious about it. Take your role seriously, follow the suggestions I've offered here, and seek the advice of mentors and colleagues. Pick their brains, compare strategies, and look for winning techniques that fit with your style.

is generally not a good choice. A carefully thought-out change for a known gain is usually a wise choice. The TOPGUN Staffex is all about identifying carefully studied curriculum changes for immediate action. So what is the value of this approach for your business? Have you ever asked your best clients about your performance goods/others? An excellent place for this conversation is lunch or dinner, on you, at a nice restaurant. Email and electronic surveys seldom provide the level of detailed feedback required for your best strategic, operational, and tactical decisions. If you say you are too busy for in-person client meetings, remember that your competition is busy too—busy trying to steal your clients. So give those client debrief meetings more thought. Then start scheduling them.

TOPGUN does what any successful business does to remain successful—they add value to their product, and they do it continuously. Most businesses can't duplicate TOPGUN's level of scrutiny over their daily operations, but if you can, in any way, mimic some elements of the TOPGUN approach to reviewing customer and client feed-back, you will be gaining an important tool for improving the daily operational effectiveness of your personal and team performances. And as a result, you can maximize your organization's credibility with its clients, prospects, and business partners.

My observation is that the debrief using a goods/others approach is a very powerful tool, but it is not used much in business. Defining successes and failures will improve the company performance over time. Defining the failures will also lessen the "repeat gripes." Without a consistent method of analyzing problems, mistakes can remain hid-den (and often do). This will result in your and your team's perfor-mance lagging well behind what it could be—a dangerous strategy in today's global economy.

Maximizing Team Performance

Have you ever been a member of a highly effective team in school, in sports, or earlier in your career? What did you like most about that team? Why was it effective? What did your teammates do to set the team apart? Unfortunately, that type of team excellence is rare and seldom repeated, which is a shame given the critical importance of teamwork in almost every organization today. I think this quote, from an unknown source, says it best: "The vehicle of accomplishment is fueled by teamwork."

The Navy has mastered the process of selecting and building top-performing aviation teams, such as its TOPGUN instructors, Blue Angels pilots, and combat aircrews. Their criteria for selecting team members offer all of us some keen insights into the process of find-ing the right people to do the right jobs, despite the complexity of the work required.

Answering the Toughest Questions

As a participant on several TOPGUN instructor selection boards, I can assure you that we take that selection process very seriously. We want to be certain that the five or six aviators we select annually from a list of more than forty well-qualified candidates are absolutely the best available for the job.

The Blue Angels, the Navy's elite flight demonstration team, also must select the best, most qualified aviators to fly on their wing. Each year, the Blue Angels have approximately fifty applicants for just *three* openings. I have been invited several times to fly with the Blue Angels. They are world renowned for the precision of their tight flight formations, at speeds in excess of 400 mph and altitudes below 200 feet. I have flown their whole show in the slot plane at the back of the four-plane diamond formation. The planes fly within eighteen inches of one another, from wingtip to canopy—so close that I feel like I can reach out and touch the wingtips of the planes on our wings. There is no margin for error with this low-altitude, high-speed, tight-formation flying.

U.S. Navy photo by Mass Communications Specialist 1st Class Rachel McMarr/Released.

Another group—combat aviation teams—uses the same demanding selection standards, operating under the simple premise that the best teams win. And in combat, winning is everything. You win, you live; you lose, you die.

In selecting aviators as TOPGUN instructors, Blue Angels, and combat partners, we ask three questions of all candidates. These questions establish the cornerstone of our selection process. They also guide our efforts to develop the great chemistry necessary for achieving the best possible team performance possible:

- Can I put my highest trust in you?
- Can I count on you to do the right things at the right time for the right reasons, professionally and personally, under any circumstances?
- Are you willing to live by, and be judged by, higher standards than others in your industry?

Let's begin with the issue of trust. This is the military's paramount question—in fact, in the military, the question we ask of our team members is: *Can I trust you with my life?* Trust is also the number-one element in every relationship, including with a client, a senior manager, a subordinate, a spouse, a significant other, children, family members, and friends. All meaningful relationships start with trust and require ongoing trust in order to grow. If you or your team members can't share a high level of trust, there's no way you can achieve peak performance. You might think this lack of trust could not possibly apply to you, but think again. The *Wall Street Journal* several years ago surveyed 1,200 mid-level executives from Fortune 500 companies and asked if they trusted senior management. About 75 percent of respondents replied no. That means that potentially three out of four people who work for you don't trust you. Yikes!

How can you know whether your team trusts in you and your abilities as a decision maker? Take a page out of the TOPGUN playbook and ask your people—anonymously, if you want accurate answers—whether they trust you, other senior executives who work for you, and their teammates. And since maximizing performance is our number-one goal, also ask about what you and your senior executives can do to improve the team's trust. Ask these questions at least twice a year. Compare results from year to year to find out how you are doing, which direction you are going, and whether you're satisfied with the results.

Without a network of trusted relationships, your team won't have an infrastructure in place to achieve peak performance when things get tough at work. Sure, you might bull your way ahead for a time, leaving any number of broken relationships strewn along your path. But this whatever-it-takes-to-get-ahead approach eventually catches up with everyone who tries it. If your team doesn't trust you and each other, they won't be there when you need them the most. You may not realize you've lost them until a crisis erupts.

Reliability is an essential element of trust, and it lies at the core of our second question: *Can I count on you to do the right thing at the right time for the right reasons, no matter what the circumstances?* So how do you build the reliability of your team?

We all know the right things to do, particularly in business, with proper ethics, protocol, and procedures to follow. Again, this is not about whatever it takes to make the deal. We all have been involved in those deals, or situations, when we think long and hard about choice A compared with choice B. You know that feeling—something about what you're planning to do at work just doesn't feel right. That funny feeling deep inside your gut is your conscience sending a message. Consider the following:

- Do you or any member of your team falsely tell clients that you can provide a product or service at a cheaper price than your competitors? Are there hidden costs with your product or service that you will reveal only if asked or only after the contract is signed?

- Are there potential flaws in your product or service that you are concealing from your clients?

- Have you been open about potential conflict-of-interest issues? Or have you remained silent about them?

We are all familiar with the mantra *buyer beware*, but is that really the message you want your team sending to clients? When clients catch on, and they always will, do you think they'll continue to do business with you? Do you think they will tell anyone about a bad experience with your group? All clients talk, and statistics indicate that they tell at least fourteen people about a negative business experience.

Do you make promises you cannot keep? Do you allow teammates to make knowingly false statements to clients or twist the facts provided to clients to serve your purpose? If you and your team are focused exclusively on making the deal or completing a project—whatever form that deal or project may take—you aren't going to be able to build your team's reliability over time, and that will stand in the way of any attempts at ongoing performance improvement.

You can rationalize that you need the money, bills at home are due, you want to make quarterly figures look good, or your standing in the office may suffer. However, if you answered yes to any of the previous questions, you may wish to reevaluate how you do business and how effectively you are leading your team toward maximized performance and results.

That brings us to the third and final question that can guide you as you work to build a top-performing team: *Are you willing to live by and be judged by a higher set of standards than everyone else?*

TOPGUN instructors, Blue Angels aviators, and Aces are well known and respected in military aviation. You and your team won't be able to command that kind of respect if you aren't willing to hold yourself to the highest standards. Think about it. By your second day on the job, you're becoming known to company coworkers, clients, and prospects. How do you want them to view you? That all depends on the professional standards you have set for your team—and on the standards each of you has set for your personal and professional lives. Those standards must reflect core values, such as ethics, honesty, committed effort, fair treatment, and more. Individually, these standards are personal decisions, but as a team, you all need to share a core set of standards that support congruence between what you say and what you do—standards that result in behavior and outcomes you are happy to subject to any level of scrutiny.

This isn't about dealing in the gray area, where you think your behavior may vary, depending on the situation. It's about one set of rules—the right rules—all the time. The benefit is loyal, solid relationships. Clients reward trust with repeat business. Senior management rewards trust with promotions. Teammates reward trust with consistent, strong job performances. You get a clearer path to maximizing your peak performance under pressure.

Do you and your team earn the highest levels of trust? Can you be counted on to do the right things, at the right times, for the right reasons—no matter what? Are you all willing to be judged by the highest standards in your field or industry? These three tough questions are just as valid to the strong performance and chemistry among you and your team as they are for TOPGUN instructors, Blue Angels aviators, and combat partners. In essence, the questions are asking you to establish your integrity, and as the saying goes, "With integrity, nothing else matters. Without integrity, nothing else matters." If you adopt an approach to business and team leadership centered on those three essential questions, you may sometimes lose a deal or make slightly less money than you might have by cutting the corners of your integrity. Yet, in the long run—and that's the only way to look at your career—you'll be miles ahead of those who let money alone drive their days. To develop truly valuable business relationships, you need to be certain that you and your team set the standard for the kind of integrity that lies at the heart of all peak performance.

Putting a Premium on People Skills

While assigned to TOPGUN, I helped organize a nine-month study that analyzed the components of successful and unsuccessful student aircrew teams going through the TOPGUN course. We identified a number of reasons for success and failure.

The leading factor in approximately 70 percent of the losing dogfights we studied was not a lack of team talent but a lack of team chemistry—measured by how well the aircrews worked together as a unit. That's why TOPGUN stresses the importance of picking the right combat teams with the best chemistry. If the chemistry among the crews going through the TOPGUN course isn't right, TOPGUN expects the aircrews to sit down together after hours, talk it out, identify the problems, and fix them. We also expect the student teams to keep working on their chemistry to get it right and make it better for one simple reason. TOPGUN's emphasis is always on airborne results—first in training, then in combat. We know from experience that the best teams really do win. I also have learned that many times, the best team chemistry comes from teams whose members demonstrate the strongest people skills.

People skills should play a major role in any team selection process. All other factors being equal, TOPGUN looks for future instructors with the best interpersonal qualities. Here are some of the questions they consider about the candidates:

DON'T KILL YOUR PEOPLE SKILLS

Here's a brief word of caution: people skills can fade under a frantic, nonstop pace that lasts week after week and month after month. For TOPGUN and the Blue Angels, the risk of burnout is always a concern. TOPGUN implements a two-week reduced schedule four times a year between classes. This gives the instructors a chance to regroup, catch their breath, and get recharged and ready for the next class. You should do the same from time to time. How will you know that it's time to take a break? Among other things, when that face staring back at you in the mirror first thing in the morning (or each one looking at you from across the conference table in meetings) has the last-mile-in-the-marathon look. Burnout is a very real, insidious hazard in many lines of work today and shouldn't be ignored. As a company or department leader, it's your responsibility to be on the alert for its signs and to take immediate corrective action when you see them.

- Will they praise in public and correct in private?
- How approachable are they?
- Can they state important points articulately and move on?
- Can they disagree without being disagreeable?
- Are they willing to flag phoniness when necessary?
- How well do they listen?
- Are they willing to admit their mistakes?
- Do they mind sharing the credit for jobs well done?
- Can they stand their ground with tough decisions?
- Are they flexible and open minded?
- Are they fun to hang out with?
- Do they have a sense of humor? Can they laugh at themselves?
- Do they conduct themselves with credibility?

These questions have proven over time to be fundamental ingredients in Naval Aviation's uniquely successful selection system. Since TOPGUN's founding in 1969, program leaders have used these questions to help select approximately 250 instructors from a field of more than 2,000 well-qualified candidates. Since 1946, the Blue Angels have relied on the same types of questions to choose 260 aviators from the 3,400 qualified candidates under consideration. In both groups, almost all of those selected exceeded the rigorous daily performance expectations of TOPGUN and the Blue Angels. All candidates for these military flying jobs have superior aviation skills, but not all have the same level of people skills. Like you, we at TOPGUN want the best of both worlds.

TOPGUN and Blue Angel teams work together for twelve to fifteen hours a day, six days a week, for three years. During that period, they spend much more time with each other than with their own families. Your team at work may not be engaged in the same level of togetherness, but its ability to achieve peak performance depends on the same types of interpersonal skills. To build and maintain strong team chemistry, remember to select bright, well-qualified candidates with strong people skills, and then work to continue building those skills among all team members.

Instilling Confidence

Because it is a military training program, you might expect that TOPGUN's training program is focused tightly on teaching proper airborne tactics. But at TOPGUN, an equally important area of focus is on building confidence—a quality that any leading executive, athlete, or person at the top of his or her profession must have in order to achieve sustained success.

In chapter 3, we talked about the importance of developing authentic self-confidence. If you want your team to achieve their top performance, it's equally important that you help them build the same level of self-confidence. A first step toward that goal is leading your team in the Peak Performance Formula element of relentless preparation. As you learned earlier, thorough preparation bolsters confidence by arming you with the tools you need to respond to the many what-ifs that can develop in almost any business day or project.

The simple act of really *listening* to and caring about your team members is another must-have tool for developing their confidence in their own performance and in you as a leader.

In any line of work, when you are more confident about the job at hand, you can tackle it in a much more determined, dedicated manner. About halfway through the TOPGUN course, most students show noticeable improvement, and that bolsters their confidence. Good decisions, now the norm, happen quicker. Situational awareness goes up. They are winning and, in many cases, dominating their dogfights against instructors. That leads to a big jump in confidence. Listen to your team, care about their progress, and help them improve. You'll grow their confidence *and* help to maximize their performance—and your own.

In TOPGUN's case, students develop confidence by learning how to fly winning dogfights every day. You can use the same approach to develop your own confidence and model it for new hires, subordinates, and others you work for and with. Project the confidence you have developed through proper project administration; through good, reliable customer service; and through prompt client/prospect follow-up. This kind of confident performance should permeate every department in every organization. If you can learn to more confidently handle your projects at work, when things get tough, your level of peak performance under pressure will immediately jump. By modeling authentic confidence, you can help others on your team work toward the same kind of ongoing performance maximization. And keep that TOPGUN model in mind. Repetition builds confidence.

Winning, Success, and Peace of Mind

We've talked a lot in this chapter about the importance of following a program of ongoing improvement, and its vital role in helping you continue to hit the highest levels of your personal and professional performance. Throughout this chapter, and this book, I have made frequent mention of the single-minded goal of the Aces—to win, every time. In combat flying, winning is the definition of success. Now, before we leave this chapter, take a moment to consider what *you* mean when you talk about success. That word means many things to many different people, but if I were to identify the one constant that links almost every definition of success, I would say "peace of mind."

That kind of success only comes to those who have made their absolute best effort to be the best they can be. But peace of mind is an elusive thing to acquire, particularly in combat. I thought about my own definition of success for many years but was not able to come up with the right words. Then a few years ago, I was invited to a presentation by UCLA's legendary former basketball coach, John Wooden. Coach Wooden's teams won seven consecutive NCAA basketball championships and ten championships over a period of twelve years. After his presentation, a member of the audience asked Wooden what he said to his players about winning and losing. The coach smiled and said he never discussed winning and losing with his players. Instead he emphasized effort. He knew that if his talented players made the effort to be the best they could be, they would win most of their games. He went on to say that, for him, success was the peace of mind that only comes through that kind of effort.

For me, a light bulb came on. Coach Wooden had just put into words a concept that I'd been thinking about for more than twenty-five years. In any area of life, *your effort to be your best results in peace of mind, which equals success.*

The Aces knew that to win most dogfights, they had to do several crucial things correctly. Their goal was always to be at their best when under peak pressure. The Aces were willing to devote every waking hour of every day to doing whatever was necessary to turn in their best performance. When the Aces went to bed at night, they never knew what was going to happen to them on the next day's mission. But they didn't worry about it and slept well. They had the satisfaction of knowing they had made the effort to be the best they could be for whatever challenges awaited them in combat.

Whatever you mean when you talk about success, remember that when you have given your best effort to be your best, you too can go to sleep at night and rest easy. You can be confident that you are as prepared as you can be to tackle whatever challenge might come your way. Like the Aces, you then will have peace of mind—the most important tool for winning in any tough, challenging, or pressure-packed situation.

Chapter Debrief

To further explore and understand how the information you've learned in this chapter relates to your peak performance, consider your answers to these questions:

Q } Do you have a plan for where you'd like to be with your company and with your career three to five years from now? How often do you review and update your plans?

1. When was the last time you updated your career plan? Is it still valid?

2. How does your current company and career development compare with what you planned? Are you satisfied? Why, or why not?

3. Do you think you will have the same job doing the same things three to five years from now? What can you do now to make sure you are in a better position then?

Your response: _____

_____

_____

_____

Q } When making an honest assessment of yourself as a leader, what are your greatest leadership strengths? How are you using them to maximize your performance? What are your biggest leadership weaknesses? How are you correcting them?

1. Think about effective leaders you worked for earlier in your career or maybe teachers or coaches who left a lasting impression on you. What made these leaders effective?

2. Why did you like being a part of their team?

3. How were they able to maintain strong leadership over time?

4. What's the biggest leadership lesson you learned from them?

5. Have you ever worked for someone who asked you to do things they wouldn't do? How did it make you feel?

6. Do you have a mentor? Why, or why not? Would you like a mentor? How could a mentor best help you?

Your response: _____

_____

_____

_____

Q } Are your most important clients, colleagues, and senior management satisfied with your daily performance? How do you know?

    1. Have you ever had a face-to-face performance assessment with one of your most important clients? What was the biggest thing you learned?

Your response: _____

_____

_____

_____

Q } Do your teammates and senior management like working with you? Why, or why not?

    1. What's the biggest thing you can do to improve your likability quotient at the workplace?

    2. Do your teammates trust you? What can you do to increase their trust? When do you plan to start?

    3. How would you rate your people skills at work? What can you do to improve those skills?

Your response: _____

_____

_____

_____

Q } As unexpected challenges emerge at work, does your confidence ever get shaken? If yes, what's your corrective action?

1. What's been your most effective technique for regaining your confidence at work?

2. Do you approach your projects and assignments at work confident that you've made the effort to be the best you can be? What can you do to improve your confidence at work?

3. What happens in your workplace to those who ooze phony confidence?

4. Who can you most depend on at crunch time in your organization? Why?

5. Do you think your teammates are comfortable depending on you in a crunch? Why, or why not? What can you do to increase your dependability quotient with them?

Your response: _____

_____

_____

_____

CHAPTER SEVEN

MAINTAINING EXCELLENCE THROUGH SELF-DISCIPLINE

"There are no points for second place."
—F-14 TOMCAT MOTTO

Throughout this book, we have examined the power of individual elements within the Peak Performance Formula, including *planning, preparation, focus, assessment,* and *improvement.* You also have learned how legendary Aces, TOPGUN students, and top decision makers everywhere leverage these elements to succeed in any competitive arena. In this chapter, we turn our attention to the Peak Performance Formula's final element, the glue that holds the entire formula together: self-discipline.

Throughout our lives, self-discipline has been our most effective tool for facing down difficult challenges. Whether we are studying, exercising, dieting, working, or following our own personal and professional standards, it's our level of self-discipline that determines our level of success. In fact, self-discipline plays a role in nearly every other element of the Peak Performance Formula. I have given it an individual place, however, to remind you of the self-discipline involved in consistently following the *entire* formula, even when you don't think you have the motivation, ability, or willingness to do so. Half-measures won't do it. You have to train yourself to apply every element of the formula if you want to reach and maintain peak performance, each time, every time, in even the most high-pressure situations.

Following the Peak Performance Formula isn't always easy. In fact, at times, it can seem as though you are being bombarded with opportunities for shortcuts and temptations to take the easy way out. In this chapter, you will learn how this final element, self-discipline, can help you avoid the most common—and performance killing—workplace ambushes. These include dealing with today's time-constrained more-with-less workplace, eliminating self-induced setbacks, and defending your core values, even as you maneuver to maximize your results. Your ability to consistently follow the formula also enables you to maintain a healthy work–life balance. As you will learn in this chapter, you can't be strong in your professional life without equally strong commitments to your family and other personal relationships.

Now let me begin this chapter by taking us back to the story that began this book, as I invite you once again into my cockpit for that last dogfight on my final combat mission over North Vietnam. As you are about to learn, the events of that desperate battle demanded that Duke and I use our self-discipline like a weapon, as we drew on every element of our training, preparation, and experience to defeat the most skilled enemy we had ever faced. As testimony to the combined fire power of the Peak Performance Formula's elements, the outcome of that dogfight says it all.

Winning With Intention

Duke and I were leaving the battle area after just having shot down two MIGs in separate, vicious dogfights. We had flown our plane and pushed ourselves to our physical limit. As we were exiting the area, we spotted yet another enemy MIG racing at us head-on. Duke pulled our F-4 Phantom jet hard into the MIG's oncoming path, very close to make sure that our adversary could not turn his plane into us and gain any tactical advantage.

However, as we passed the MIG close aboard, we realized we had made a big mistake. We had given the enemy pilot a good head-on gun shot. He capitalized on that opportunity and fired a volley from the two 23-millimeter cannons mounted under his wings. Although we should have known better, we were surprised. Nevertheless, our training had prepared us to respond; Duke immediately turned our jet hard, away and down out of the line of the MIG's barrage of bullets.

We were very familiar with the strengths and weaknesses of our F-4 Phantom and our opponent's MIG-17. Because of the Phantom's superior power, Duke quickly pulled our jet straight up 90 degrees, into what we called the extreme vertical. Our plan was to take a look, then pounce down from above. We expected to easily outclimb the MIG. Unfortunately, we were up against a formidable foe—a man some believed to have been the infamous Colonel Nguyen Toon, rumored to be North Vietnam's leading Ace, credited with thirteen U.S. kills. Whatever his real name might have been, this pilot was highly skilled and intent on shooting us down. To win this dogfight, we had to be in full command of our A-game. We couldn't hesitate, make a mistake, or allow our focus to waver, even for a moment.

We didn't know it yet, but we'd been set up. Just prior to passing this new adversary head-on for the first time, we had been turning hard to complete the shoot-down of our second MIG of that flight. We hadn't yet fully restored our lost airspeed when our adversary whizzed by. No wonder he outclimbed us. He was substantially faster when both our planes zoomed vertical. He knew that aggressive American F-4 Phantom pilots would surely relish a vertical dogfight against his MIG-17 due to the Phantom's greater power and thrust. He essentially gave us the invitation to the vertical dogfight we wanted. We eagerly, but naively, took his bait. Our enemy had his attack well under way before we ever saw him. We had failed to assess the situation carefully before acting. We were in big trouble and would have to call on all of our training and experience to win.

Our adversary quickly proved that he knew exactly what he was doing as he outclimbed us and rolled the nose of his plane on us for his vertical attack. All he had to do was continue to deny us the opportunity to regain airspeed. As our bigger jet slowed further, our opponent could force us into his "no escape zone," like a boxer backing a rival into a corner of the ring, and he would then close for the kill—a simple but effective tactic.

Realizing the enemy's rapidly improving advantage, Duke pulled our Phantom hard into the MIG, attempting to force it into a vertical overshoot. But the enemy Ace matched our turn rate perfectly; we couldn't shake him off our tail. The MIG, armed with guns and heat-seeking missiles, closed rapidly into position, then opened fire with all guns blazing. Stepping up to meet the escalating challenge, Duke immediately rolled our jet violently sideways, slicing toward the ground to avoid the bullets. We were now in a desperate spiraling dive, straight down toward the lush green countryside of North Vietnam.

A ferocious twisting, rolling, vertical dogfight ensued with our Phantom almost continually in the MIG's gun sight. Our adversary was so close I could nearly reach out and touch his plane's stubby nose. It looked like the opening of a trash barrel pointed at my cockpit.

He made all the right decisions as he relentlessly pressed for the kill. Duke and I remained focused on fighting like we'd never fought before. We knew that we had the skills, the training, and the tools for winning—the thought that we might lose never occurred to either of us. We believed that if we continued following our training, working the problem, and never letting up, this dogfight would shift our way.

Following a second rolling, vertical maneuver—called a slow-speed rolling scissors—our Phantom had "bled down" to almost 200 knots, a dangerously slow airspeed with a MIG-17 within 300 feet of us, guns blazing. This is exactly what our attacker wanted. To survive, Duke had to keep pushing our Phantom to its aerodynamic limits. We were in constant communication through inner-cockpit radio transmissions. Although I saw several other MIGs flash behind us, I noted their presence without letting them distract me. We had our hands full with this one, and we riveted our focus on him.

Our assessment of the situation told us we had two choices. One was to continue with the vertical, rolling dogfight—with our airspeed decelerating to almost zero—hoping that our attacker would somehow miss us with his remaining bullets and leave. The other was to bring the Phantom's throttles back to idle while deploying the speed brakes to force our unsuspecting enemy into a vertical overshoot. Because he had flown his MIG so well and aggressively, the first option made little sense. We knew the second option would put us in the best position to attack—and win.

As our enemy closed in to finish us, Duke abruptly yanked the throttles back to idle and deployed the speed brake. Approaching sixty degrees nose up, our Phantom rapidly decelerated well below 200 knots. Our unexpected move caught the MIG pilot completely off guard. He overshot us vertically and flew right out in front of us. In an instant, his overwhelming advantage dissolved. Realizing the enormity of his blunder, the pilot dropped the MIG's nose and dove directly for the ground, turning belly-up to us to escape. That was a big mistake.

Duke ruddered our severely buffeting, wing-stalled Phantom downward toward the enemy jet. As the Phantom's nose fell through the horizon with our attacker now fleeing in front of us, we accelerated and reestablished our turn rate. The enemy pilot then made his final mistake. While trying to get away from our now rapidly accelerating Phantom, he didn't roll his MIG to maintain sight of us. He wouldn't see the smoke trail of our missile launch, nor would he have any chance to outmaneuver it.

As we closed in on the MIG from its belly side, we realized the pilot still didn't see us. We also realized that the background of a steamy jungle could be a guidance problem for our heat-seeker missile. Duke pulled the nose of our now much faster, more maneuverable Phantom down onto the enemy jet's tailpipe and kept it there as we continued rapidly descending. With the altitude gauge unwinding furiously, Duke fired. We watched anxiously as the missile hissed away in a puff of white smoke, like a high-speed dart trained directly on the unsuspecting MIG.

The missile exploded just prior to impact, breaking off a section of the MIG's tailpipe. As we prepared to fire our last missile, the enemy jet smashed into the ground in a spectacular bright orange fireball. The pilot did not eject. Shifting our focus away from the MIG explosion, we realized how close we were to the ground. With a Herculean high-G pullout at extremely low altitude, we barely avoided hitting the jungle trees.

Duke and I later acknowledged that we were able to hold off this particularly skilled adversary because of our TOPGUN training. Our training flights had put us through the same situations we now encountered in combat and had given us the mental and technical skills necessary to respond instinctively. We were able to remain focused on our primary objectives, to maintain an ongoing assessment of our evolving situation, and to continually up our game in order to beat an incredibly skilled and determined opponent. Although we didn't think in these terms at the time, we had followed a formula that had enabled us to perform at our best and with confidence, in the fight of our lives. We made mistakes, as will you when you take on some of your most high-stakes challenges. But some mistakes, if you recognize them soon enough, are not fatal if you can take corrective action to minimize their consequences.

Now let's take a look at how falling victim to common oversights and failing to follow all elements of the Peak Performance Formula almost transformed our winning final combat mission into a fatally flawed disaster—and what lessons that experience holds for you.

Avoiding the Biggest Workplace Ambushes

President John F. Kennedy once said, "If you only focus on the past and ignore the present, you're liable to miss the future." That message holds an important truth for you, as you use the Peak Performance Formula to drive continuously better performance and results. No matter how great your individual successes might be, you can't let them distract you from the challenges ahead of you. And there will *always* be new challenges developing on your horizon. They always seem to arrive at the worst possible time. That's another lesson I learned in that last combat mission over North Vietnam.

After our last dogfight with that enemy pilot, Duke had pulled our plane's nose up into a steep climb, then began our flight to the coast, about forty miles away. I gave him a heading that I believed was a safe course back over enemy territory to our aircraft carrier. We took a moment to bask in the radiance of our victories with some excited back-and-forth chatter over our radios. No aviators in military aviation history had ever shot down three enemy jets with missiles on one mission. Yapping like two schoolboys at recess, we got caught up in the moment and took a short break from monitoring our radar, electronic warfare displays, and radios. Although we saw two enemy jet fighters orbiting well below us at treetop level, we ignored them too. Worse yet, we quit scanning the sky for other threats. We were too busy celebrating.

We also ignored the proper tactics needed to fly a safe egress. We were in a wings-level climb, flying about 200 mph slower than we had trained. We removed our oxygen masks to wipe our sweat-drenched faces. We were still talking back and forth about that last dogfight when, from out of nowhere, we were stunned by a brilliant white-orange flash and a deafening explosion that bounced our Phantom like heavy turbulence. Then came the screech of tearing metal along the side of our plane. One look outside told us that we had been hit by a SAM.

Our plane kept climbing, but as I looked out over my left shoulder, I spotted small fires along the aft side of our left wing. I also saw that those two enemy MIGs had left their treetop orbits and were racing toward us. Duke reported that our F-4 Phantom was losing the hydraulic fluid that powers the plane's flight controls. We somehow had to save our remaining hydraulic fluid to stay airborne long enough to reach the coast, still twenty miles away.

Both of us had read in *Approach Magazine*, a Navy Safety Center aviation publication, about an F-4 Phantom pilot who had kept his plane flying after it was hit by a SAM that caused a similar catastrophic hydraulic failure. To save remaining hydraulic fluid, that pilot used his rudder pedals to control his plane's flight path through a series of vertical maneuvers aimed at keeping his jet airborne. We knew our only chance was to use the very techniques outlined in that article to guide our barely controllable Phantom to a safer area for ejection.

We now were about ten miles from the coast. Our plane went through a series of ever-wider vertical, twisting, rolling loops that unfolded almost exactly as we had read about in that article. Relying only on the rudders enabled us to exert some control over our wildly rolling, burning jet. We used this technique for what seemed like an eternity—in truth, about four minutes—as we approached the coast. Our momentary loss of focus had landed us in a life-threatening situation, but the techniques we had learned in that magazine gave us invaluable information when we needed it most. We had regained our self-discipline and our focus. We also had called on our relentless preparation, assessed the situation, and let our training take over. Now we had to put all of our effort and renewed focus into our next steps. We couldn't panic, clutch up, or let our emotions in the moment cause us to make another mistake. Our lives depended on us doing the right things, right then. There would be no second chance.

Unexpected problems and sudden catastrophes are not limited to combat aviators. The potential for mishaps and monumental setbacks in your workplace is ever present and ready to attack you, usually at the worst possible time. Chief among the workplace ambushes that you will face are fear, self-inflicted setbacks, and threats to your core values. Let's take a look at your disciplined use of all elements of the Peak Performance Formula to see how they can help you avoid these ambushes and survive any type of attack in the high-pressure combat zone of your office, business, or industry.

Facing Down Fears

Each year, I give approximately forty speeches to mid- and upper-level executives across the United States. A portion of each speech deals with the mistakes we made in the minutes leading up to our jet getting hit by that unobserved SAM. I explain how I felt in the cockpit over enemy territory as we lost control of our plane. I always describe my feelings as the outer stratosphere of tension, anxiety, stress, and fear—all normal feelings for someone in that situation—and how my training and self-discipline helped me continue functioning effectively in spite of them. I remind my audience that they too can call on the system provided in the Peak Performance Formula to escape the negative impact of the ever-present tension, anxiety, and stress of today's workplace. Once emotions gain the upper hand, your chances for reaching peak performance plummet. The 4 percent of fighter pilots who became Aces had disciplined themselves to remain focused on flying their plane, even when it seemed impossible to do. That's one of the secrets of how they became Aces.

Believe me, I felt great fear in the cockpit of that burning, barely controllable jet. I had to try my utmost not to vomit or mess my pants and to manage the involuntary shaking of my arms and legs. We were losing control of our plane. Enemy jets were closing in to finish us. We still had several miles to go before reaching the coast. We both knew if we survived an ejection over land, we'd be captured by the enemy and become prisoners of war. Our best chance for rescue was an ejection over water. Meanwhile, the fire in my cockpit was snaking its way closer to me. I was strapped tightly to my ejection seat and at the mercy of those flames. The cockpit was hot and so smoky that I had to lean as far forward as I could to read the flight gauges. But we could not panic. Our training and preparation offered the tools we needed to survive; we just had to call on our discipline to use them.

Duke was doing his best to control the plane while dealing with the same smoke and fire. I served as a talking instrument panel, calling out over the intercockpit radio our Phantom jet's airspeed, altitude, nose position, and updates on the approaching enemy fighters. The timing

USE THE TOOLS AVAILABLE TO YOU

Take a lesson from my experiences, and don't ignore the advice and information available to you in professional publications. Read the industry and trade magazines related to your work, and keep on top of national print and online publications. I quickly scan five newspapers each morning and four or five business magazines each week. My favorite business publications are the *Harvard Business Review, The Economist,* and *Selling Power.* These materials, whether in print or online versions, offer excellent insights on how other professionals in your field deal with the same types of challenges you face every day at work.

The digital age has made it possible for us to take advantage of an abundance of resources for industry updates, insights, product reviews, and lessons learned. Much of this information is presented by well-known upper-level leaders, decision makers, and managers who write about new challenges they face, what they are doing about them, what's working, not working, and why. They offer expert insights about your industry with emphasis on the changes they see coming. As you have learned, to do your best under pressure, you have to constantly look for ways to improve your performance. What you read today may prove vital later, when you're hit with an unexpected crisis.

of our rudder-rolls and dive recoveries was based on the accuracy of my calls. I remember telling myself to slow down, get a grip on myself, sound calm on the radio, and concentrate on doing what I was trained to do—something difficult but not impossible.

At the top of our fourth loop as we approached the coastline, we completely lost control of our jet. It slammed us hard sideways and then snap-rolled into an inverted spin. We were immediately squashed against the top of our canopies, flying at 180 mph, upside down, at approximately 12,000 feet over the enemy's harbor. A blast furnace of fire suddenly erupted inside my cockpit. It was time for me to do the last job—to eject us out of this hell-hole before we were burned alive.

With flames licking all around me, I pressed my body down from the canopy with my left hand and got two fingers of my right hand down onto the ejection handle mounted on my seat. A powerful surge of adrenalin certainly gave me a blast of strength to reach it— in trying to repeat the maneuver in ejection seat simulator training, I've never been able to get my hand closer than a foot away from that handle. But I made it that day, when our lives hung in the balance.

I talk about this event in the presentations I make to business leaders and organizations interested in maximizing their peak performance under pressure as they respond to growing threats in their own industry or workplace. I have always been highly motivated to share the lessons I learned with others who are coping with tough, stressful situations. I hope that my experiences can help them understand that surviving a vicious attack doesn't require a miracle. But it does demand a disciplined response—one you can leverage by staying on track and using the skills, tools, and experience you've acquired. Self-discipline is your strongest weapon against the fears and distractions that confront you during tough times. It gives you the determination to stick with the plan, remember your preparation, maintain your focus, and keep moving forward in the face of *any* attack.

Eliminating Self-Inflicted Setbacks

In combat, it wasn't only the enemy and his tactics that caused the Aces tension and anxiety; the way they responded to their enemy's actions also determined the Aces' level of stress. Aces learned how to reduce their stress reactions at the most critical times by using quick *reaction* flying compared with the longer *analytical* flying. The Aces were locked in on each move as the dogfight unfolded and, as a result of their thorough preparation, they responded in a split second to every development that unfolded. They almost always made good decisions at decisive times.

What's the connection for you? Admittedly the stakes are very different when comparing a day at the office with a day flying over enemy territory. But the Aces offer a valuable lesson that's universal. Think about those deals you almost closed but didn't. Or new clients or business opportunities you almost brought in, only to have them slip away. What's the

FINDING A ROCK-SOLID FOUNDATION

There will be times at work when you've done everything humanly possible to effect a favorable outcome with an important project, a major customer, or a tricky assignment. You probably will have spent a lot of your time and company resources on this effort. As you await the outcome, you're nervous and can feel yourself getting wired even tighter. Your stomach twists into ever-tightening knots. These emotions are similar to those the Aces felt before launching on their combat missions.

The Aces literally flew in and out of the valley of death. Not all who took off on a combat mission returned. They saw death and destruction all around them every day, and some drew on their spirituality to help them through those times. They didn't know what the future held for them in combat any more than you know what the future holds for your life. But many of us believe that our future is part of a greater spiritual plan. When our lives turn totally upside down, as happens to all of us on occasion, it's okay to be afraid—and to fall back on our spiritual beliefs and core values for guidance and comfort. Now I'm not talking about praying to close a deal or win new business or make more money. I'm talking about examining our most important personal beliefs to find the wisdom to make a tough decision and to get all of the facts before jumping to conclusions. I'm talking about relying on our convictions to help us find the courage to do the right things at the right time, no matter how much pressure we are under to compromise our ethics. When we're guided by our deepest core values, we can muster the perseverance necessary to hang in there and keep working through a tough problem to find the right solution. That's how we can face down our fear and keep moving forward, no matter what the future holds.

I felt varying degrees of fear in most of my combat missions and asked God to give me courage. I slowly began to realize that courage in combat is not about the absence of fear. Rather, it's about going forward and doing a good job *in spite* of your fear. I found my own religious beliefs to be a great source of comfort flying combat and later in life navigating through the many unexpected challenges at work and at home. Your core beliefs, values, and convictions can give you the same kind of rock-solid foundation and ongoing guidance as your own future unfolds.

unvarnished reason why you failed?

Many senior executives I interviewed admitted that, when coping with problems at work, their difficulties often began with simple oversights or missteps, then doubled as the decision makers hesitated, delayed corrective action, or made weak decisions. These are self-inflicted problems that your self-discipline can help you avoid.

A fellow in our town runs a hazardous materials removal company. His business directives—which he wrote and signed—include specific requirements that all of his employees must wear exposure suits on the job. Recently, he showed up at a hazardous materials job site wearing shorts and a golf shirt. His employees were wearing exposure suits—as he had directed. When the inspector from the Environmental Protection Agency (EPA) arrived at the site, he saw the company owner standing there in casual attire and immediately shut down the job and suspended the company's license, pending a complete investigation. Now *there* is a huge, self-inflicted problem.

Almost every day at TOPGUN, the students get a heavy dose of corrective input on their performance. Those who take immediate corrective action are usually rewarded with a jump in airborne performance. The few who quibble, offer excuses, hesitate, or don't take corrective action tend to continue performing poorly. If their performance doesn't soon improve, they are asked to leave.

What about you? Do you pay your daily preparation dues, such as writing your priority to-do list and thinking through what important phone calls to make? Do you work to create simple plans with measurable goals, and then regularly take the time to assess your performance against those goals? The Aces' solution to the unpredictability of combat was to train hard, prepare realistically, and then to use their self-discipline to follow the system they had learned to win. That's how they were able to perform brilliantly in a crisis.

If you don't exercise the same kind of self-disciplined approach—consistently following the Peak Performance Formula, applying the tools and skills it provides you, and correcting problems immediately and effectively—you put yourself on course for average performance *at best*. Mediocre performance is a self-inflicted problem. If you're fighting against yourself, you can't win.

Defending Core Values

One of the keys to making a difference in your life, and the lives of the people you work so hard to influence every day, is having the self-discipline to remain true to your core values. With today's mounting pressures from multiple sources to do whatever it takes to make the deal or finish the project, our values and ethics are under constant attack. I'd like to present the following points for your consideration.

First, the work you do must matter—to you, your team, and your senior leadership. Aces truly love their work. Every one of the fighter pilots I flew with and against during my career was absolutely hooked on being a fighter pilot. They loved almost everything about their job. It was easy for them to bring unlimited motivation, enthusiasm, love of flying, and self-confidence to work every day. Nothing was staged with them. Those deep-rooted feelings made it easier to maintain their discipline and remember the ideas, values, and training that had prepared them to turn in their best performance during times of peak pressure. Of course, parts of the fighter pilot's job, such as inspections, standing watches, non-aviation training, and paperwork, are tedious. But the goods—flying jet fighters off aircraft carriers—far outweigh the others.

If you struggle to maintain the core values and standards that guide your approach to work, stop to ask yourself this important question: Do you like your job? What about your team members— do they seem to like their jobs? According to a recent study published by the Conference Board, a not-for-profit business group composed of 1,200 corporations in sixty countries, approximately 55 percent of the U.S. workforce does not like their jobs. At the time of its release, that figure represented a twenty-three-year low—a sobering statistic for those in leadership positions. It's difficult, if not impossible, for your people to embrace your ideas, plans, and initiatives with negative job feelings.

In the executive interviews I've conducted, I get substantial feedback on this lack of employee job satisfaction. It appears to be increasing across all company types and geographic sectors of the country. According to a study in the *Harvard Business Review*, 25 percent of employees plan to leave their jobs within the next twelve months, and 12 percent are now seeking work elsewhere. You may say, "Let them leave!" But what if it's a top performer who wants to join your biggest competitor? That study indicates the first to leave are usually your innovators, risk takers, and future leaders.

Here are two practices I've observed among companies that consider improving employee job satisfaction and retaining top performers as being central to maintaining their organizational core values:

1. Scheduling more frequent all-hands meetings and inter-department communications sessions to talk about setting up a more employee-friendly work environment—they're soliciting employee input, are serious about it, *and they follow up.*

2. Bringing in outside speakers and firms to survey and train all employees—they emphasize communications, teamwork, ethics, and leadership, and they solicit employee input, are serious about it, *and they follow up.*

Now for a second point about maintaining your core values: You must demonstrate a strong respect and appreciation for the people you work for and with. Most fighter pilots can't wait to get to work, and they particularly enjoy hanging out with their squadron mates. I've been assigned to eight fighter squadrons in my career, and many of the unique characters I shared those assignments with are still my close, personal friends. We stay in touch, spend holidays and vacations together, and socialize regularly. About forty of us meet for breakfast once a month in San Diego, and about thirty of us play golf there every week.

So how did these fighter pilots become such good friends? They respected each other as professionals, liked each other as people, and appreciated the courage they displayed as aviators. Those components of respect, liking, and appreciation were earned and re-earned every day with their actions, as they remained true to their core values and ignored everything else. Showing respect and appreciation for your team members, colleagues, and organization is a simple but effective strategy for staying on track. It demands a certain level of self-discipline, but it can improve the performance of any decision maker or team.

Finally, money cannot be your sole motivator for achieving peak performance. Most fighter pilots can't believe they get paid for the privilege of flying high-performance jet fighters. If the truth be known, many would fly for free, and others would pay for the opportunity. The point is that money won't be enough to continually push your performance. There's nothing wrong with making money—that's what business is all about. But you can't attain lasting success if you fail to maintain your ethics and core values in the pursuit of money. Systematically following the elements of the Peak Performance Formula will help you in both efforts.

Maintaining Strength Through Balance: Three Keys

This book has presented a lot of information for your consideration, but where to begin? You're faced with similar questions every day in your work as a decision maker, and most of those questions have to do with change. What to change? When? What gets cut back? By how much? What gets added, eliminated, or shifted to another team? With all the uncertainty in today's choppy economy, these tough questions are even more difficult to answer.

Many experts across a variety of professions all agree that without change, there is no progress. In our fiercely competitive global economy, if you stay the same, you're probably falling behind. In this book, we have talked about a number of positive changes you can achieve to ramp up your performance in even the most trying circumstances. But implementing change requires your highest levels of self-discipline. Now I'd like to present three final points as your guide for deciding the best takeaway changes you can work toward—three "golden keys" that can help you open the door to a more balanced, happy, productive life.

Be an Optimist

Warren Buffett, once the world's richest man, with a net worth of greater than $68 billion before giving more than half of it to charity, was asked what he thought of today's unpredictable economy. He replied:

- "If you were born in the United States of America, you've already won the world lottery."
- "We in the United States are workers and innovators, and we work overtime."

- "No one knows what the economy will look like when we come out of this current cycle. But I believe it will be better than ever."

- "What will happen to you five years from now depends on what you're doing today."

It's hard not to note the observation of an executive as successful as Warren Buffett. His words are filled with hope and optimism. Remember that metaphor of the glass being half-empty or half-full? What you see in your glass depends on how you look at it. Sure, you could think of ten things you dislike about your job and be on mark. You also could think about ten things you like about your job and still be on mark. How your glass looks to you depends on what you're doing to it.

Are you an optimist or a pessimist? I've met more than 100 Aces from America, Germany, Japan, Great Britain, and Israel. Many became my good friends. All were brimming with optimism (and self-confidence). These Aces weren't looking at the world through rose-colored lenses. They were genuinely grateful that their glass of life was almost always more than half-full. They were happy, upbeat, and excited about the future. Most were in their late seventies or early eighties when I first met them. All had lived full lives and had been through personal ups and downs—the death of a spouse, severe illness, failing health. Because of their optimism, they remained remarkably upbeat. Optimism isn't an accident; it's a discipline.

You too can choose how you look at your workplace challenges with all those gritty issues we've discussed. Many psychologists agree: *Your most effective tool in dealing with problems at work is a good, positive attitude.* It's easy to see the dark side of every issue. Maintaining a positive attitude takes self-discipline.

Be Kind

Let me tell you about something that I experienced several years ago—an unexpected, life-changing event I'll always remember.

I live in San Diego, California, about one mile from the Pacific Ocean. Most nights, I go to bed between 8:30 and 9:00 p.m., and by 4:15 a.m., I'm wide awake and ready to go. So I'm out of the house by 4:30 every morning for my four-mile jog along the beach, hugging the tide line. The white, foamy surf from the rolling waves licks the shore with a never-ending rumble.

While jogging, I watch with fascination as the dark night sky starts to lighten. About forty-five minutes before sunrise, the early morning sky above the Pacific puts on a dazzling display of light featuring a beautiful mixture of blue-gray, pink, orange, and yellow— all reflecting off the white foamy waves. It is breathtaking. On some mornings, a full moon hanging in the western sky bathes the beach and cliffs in silver as nature's spectacular predawn light show begins. Often I am the only one on the beach, before the first surfers arrive.

A few years ago, I began to notice a beautiful multimillion-dollar house on the oceanfront, basking in the early morning sunlight, with a torn American flag flapping from a white pole outside its front door. Each morning as I jogged by, I hoped the people living there would notice how badly the flag was damaged and do something about it. But for several weeks, it only continued to become more ripped and tattered by the ocean wind.

That ticked me off. I kept thinking that I didn't risk my life so many times in combat to see this. I felt tempted to leave a curt note at the doorstep. Something like: *Hey people, how about showing some respect for our nation's flag.* Instead, I went to the flag store in town and bought a brand new American flag. The next morning I left it on the doorstep with a note that said:

> Dear Friend:
>
> Please accept this gift of our country's flag from someone who loves our country, I'm sure, as much as you do.
>
> Sincerely,
> Bill Driscoll

The next day when I came home from work, my wife told me I had a phone message on our answering machine. Here's what I heard:

> Bill Driscoll, my name is Barbara North [I'm not using her real name, here, of course]. Thank you so much for the beautiful American flag. I just love it. My late husband passed away suddenly, several months ago. One of the last things he did before he died was to put up our family's flag. I haven't been out of the house often since he passed away, but I went outside earlier today to put up your beautiful new flag. Thank you so much.

I was *stunned*. I explained the story to my wife. I also thanked the good Lord that I didn't follow my first impulse to open my big mouth.

Many people you deal with every day at work also are struggling privately with painful life issues: a sudden illness, a family separation, a pending divorce, a troubled teenager, financial problems, a family member's alcohol or drug addiction. As the Greek philosopher Plato wisely advised back in 457 BC, "Be kind, for everyone you meet is fighting a hard battle."

Be Grateful

Life is a balancing act. Being disciplined and doing your best isn't just a matter of devoting yourself to your job. Take a look at this picture:

These are my kids, Megan and Mike, back when they were young-sters. If you have children, let me remind you of a fact that I always mention during my presentations—kids are six years old or eight years old only once. Be very careful with what you decide to cancel or postpone with them. You can't go back and re-attend a missed little league or soccer game. Some things in life are very special, and many times we just don't know how special they are until they're gone. Your kids' childhood is one. Remember, to your kids, these are the good old days. Their memories of you and them, which last a lifetime, are being formed today.

While we're on the topic of family, here's a picture of my lovely wife, Barbara.

As I write this, we have been married for thirty-three years. Sure, we've had our differ-ences. But the goods far out-weigh the others. It's been said that a happy marriage is a good conversation cut too short. I certainly agree with that. Barbara has always been there for those life-defining challenges, worries, and problems. She is the greatest, most fascinating, amazing, and loyal person I've ever met. When thinking about her, I'm reminded of what my French-Canadian grandmother once told me many years ago about rela-tionships: "If you're with the right person, when you're happy, you're twice as happy, and when you're sad, you're only half as sad." That's what's happened to me with this remarkable woman I was very priv-ileged to marry.

The most important thing you'll ever have to help you get through the tension, anxiety, and stress of everyday life—whether you're flying jet fighters in combat or trying to get through a tough day on the job—are good, supportive relationships with your family and friends. Be very grateful for those relationships. Nourish them. Cherish them. Never take them for granted. They're the best stress-reduction asset you'll ever have. And they'll always be there for you during your toughest times at work and at home. Like any invaluable asset, however, good relationships aren't a given; if you want to make them as strong as they can be, you have to invest in them with your time and attention. These are the things in life that endure and are worth your investment. At times, that investment can demand discipline, focus, planning, and effort similar to what you must summon to meet your most daunting business challenges.

Psychologists tell us that one of the keys to good mental health involves the ability to adapt to the pressures of your changing workplace. As mentioned earlier, I flew 170 combat missions. I expected them to be tough. Expect your work to be tough, too. Multiple pressures and challenges at work will inevitably collide. Expect things to be pressure-packed from time to time, and when it happens, you won't be surprised or thrown off course. This applies whether you work for someone else or yourself. The Peak Performance Formula you have learned about in this book can be your strongest tool for adaptability, by helping you perform at your best through any workplace challenge, when nothing but your best will do.

When you have mastered the self-discipline necessary to follow the elements of the formula we've talked about in this book, take a moment to congratulate yourself! You will have removed a huge source of tension, anxiety, and stress from your workday and your life. You also will have put yourself in a much better position to control your workday rather than allowing it to control you. That's the way the Aces approached their work, and the way TOPGUN trains all of its combat aviators to approach their missions. Like them, your ability to apply the tools and techniques for achieving peak performance under pressure will make you a winner—every time, no matter what.

Chapter Debrief

Here are some questions to consider as you review the information you've learned in this chapter:

Q} Do you consider yourself an expert in your field?

1. Are you satisfied with your knowledge of all aspects of your job? What areas, if you knew more about them, would have the most positive impact on improving your performance? What are you doing to increase your knowledge in your chosen field?

2. Are you keeping up with the professional publications and other written resources that can make you better at your work? If you aren't reading them now, when do you plan to start?

3. How do you rate your performance at work when the pressure on you to get the job done is the greatest? Before reading this book, what had you done to improve your performance under pressure?

4. How do you think those you work with rate your performance under pressure? Why? Do you think they like working with you during those times? Why, or why not?

Your response: _____

_____

_____

_____

Q} Have you ever analyzed the factors responsible for choosing your career?

1. Why did you select your industry as your career? Knowing what you know now, would you make the same career selection today? Why, or why not? What would you select instead?

2. What prompted you to go to work for your current organization? (Remember, money is not the first answer.) What do you like most about your job? What do you like least about it? What are you doing about it? Knowing what you know now, would you pick the same company again? Why, or why not? If you could speak in strict confidence to a friend thinking about going to work for your company, what would you tell your friend?

3. Knowing what you know now, would you select the same company today? If not, what company would you select today?

4. On a scale of 1–10, how would you grade your self-discipline at work? What are you doing to improve it? When do you plan to start? What self-discipline index score do you plan to have one year from now? How are you going to achieve this score? How will you know if you achieved it?

5. How would you evaluate your ability to make good decisions during stressful times at work? Where would you rate your decision making during stressful times: *good, fair,* or *poor*? Why? What changes could you make that would improve your decision making under pressure?

6. How would you rate your attitude at work? Do you think others you work with enjoy being around you? Why, or why not? When thinking about your job, your career, and your company, do you see yourself as an optimist or a pessimist? How do you think others see you? What are you doing to improve your attitude at work?

Your response: _____

_____

_____

_____

 Have you been able to implement an acceptable work–family balance? Why, or why not? What needs to change to provide you with a better work–family balance?

1. Do you spend sufficient time with your family? Why, or why not? What one change could you make at work that would give you more family and free time? When do you plan to implement this change?

Your response: _____

_____

_____

_____

A SIMPLE PREMISE

*"What lies behind us and what lies ahead of us
are tiny matters compared to what lies within us."*

—RALPH WALDO EMERSON

The early morning meeting scheduled for ninety minutes was creeping toward its two-hour mark, with no end in sight. Cramped in an uncomfortable chair, bored stiff, I looked around the stuffy room full of people and discretely stretched my stiff legs as I considered how I would have to adjust my already full schedule to compensate for this overrun. Suddenly, I felt an intense pain shoot up from my stomach and lock onto my chest, then grow into a vice-like pressure.

As my pain intensified, the room began tilting sideways. I felt exhausted, but I couldn't just close my eyes and go to sleep while sitting in front of a roomful of people. I tried to focus, to stay conscious until whatever was happening to me had passed. Then the room rolled upside-down and I was surrounded by an inky blackness. The next thing I knew, four burly paramedics from the local fire department were hovering over me. I had been unconscious for almost ten minutes. One paramedic asked me to sit up with his help, but when I tried to do it, the room started spinning again, and that inky-black darkness returned. The paramedic saw my eyes rolling erratically, and eased me back down onto the floor. I heard one of the paramedics say, "His pulse is 20 and dropping. I think we're losing him." *What?* I thought. *They're talking about me? I'm not ready for this!*

When I swam back to the surface, I was on a stretcher, oxygen mask and IV line in place, and being loaded into an ambulance. When I told the paramedics which hospital I used, they dismissed it as being too far away. "We don't have time," I heard someone say. "He might not make it." As the paramedics continued to talk, I realized that they believed I had suffered a major heart attack and they wanted the nearest cardiologist ready to operate as soon as we arrived.

The ambulance ride was surreal. I'd never been in one before. As I faded in and out of consciousness, I felt as though I was watching the whole scene unfold in a poor-quality home video that I could only view through a tiny hole. As I heard the paramedics discussing my chances of making it to the hospital, I thought about Barbara, my wife of thirty-three years, the most remarkable, loyal, and amazing person I've ever met. I tried to remember every detail of the last time I saw her earlier that morning. You know what it's like—rushing out the door for another hectic workday, juggling briefcase and coffee, thinking about that day's upcoming problems. Had I known what was in store for me on this workday, that's not how that last good-bye would have gone.

And what about my two kids—Michael, twenty-six, a paramedic himself, and Megan, twenty-four, a recent college graduate who had just started her first real job. Had I done enough to get them ready for life's challenges? What did we say to each other the last time we were together? That's all I could think about as the ambulance raced to the hospital. The sound of the paramedics' ongoing conversation became mere background noise, although I did hear one of them use the words "massive heart attack."

When we arrived at the hospital, the doctors were waiting. I was wheeled into a pre-op room, where nurses hooked me up to a cluster of high-tech heart-monitoring machines, then quickly conducted an EKG along with a number of other tests. I asked a nurse to please call my wife and tell her what had happened. Then the scramble was over, and I was left alone for a few minutes, listening to the beeps, hums, and buzz of the equipment attached to my body. So what did I do? The same thing millions of people have done while lying in a hospital bed waiting for emergency surgery necessary to save their life; I prayed. Then I began asking myself big questions: Was this my time to go? Would I see my remarkable wife again? I wanted to tell her, one last time, that I loved her and thank her, again, for all she had done for me and the family. I thought about our relationship. It hadn't been perfect—we'd had real problems and challenges to deal with, just like everyone else. But whenever things got tough, I had always reminded myself that the *goods* of our relationship far outnumbered the *others*.

Then, several nurses scurried back into the room to retrieve my test results. I asked one of them for my pulse readout, and she said it was approaching 55 beats per minute. She also told me that my EKG results were normal, but the cardiologist had ordered more tests. When I asked what was going to happen next, she told me the doctors needed to review all test results before deciding. After turning down my request for water—with possible surgery looming, I couldn't eat or drink anything—the nurse told me that my wife was on her way. Then the room emptied again, leaving me alone with my thoughts.

Interestingly enough, as I lay there looking back over my life, not a thought about my business and military accomplishments entered the picture. I couldn't think of anything but my family and friends. I felt an overwhelming fatigue, but sleep was impossible. As I felt the blood pressure cuff periodically inflate and deflate, and I heard the wall clock's seconds ticking away, I turned the same questions over and over in my mind. How had this happened to me? How would I live my life differently if I survived?

Then I heard a nurse's greeting returned by a very familiar voice—my wife had arrived. The nurse pulled back the curtain surrounding my bed, and there was Barbara, with *that smile*. As she leaned over to kiss me, my eyes watered. If Barbara was nervous or scared, she hid it well. She asked me what had happened, and the nurse told her the doctor would be in to provide the details. We held hands. I must have told her at least twenty times how great it was to see her. We both lost track of time. Then, a stern-looking man in a long, white coat walked in and introduced himself as my doctor. He said I had suffered a vasovagal syncope, a fainting episode which can have symptoms similar to those of a heart attack. It was most likely caused by a combination of fatigue, overly vigorous exercise, dehydration, a stuffy room, and that prolonged stretch. He wanted to keep me in the hospital for further tests, but if the results were negative, he expected to discharge me that evening. He suggested that Barbara go home and bring me a change of clothes.

A short time later, I was again alone with my thoughts, the green digital displays, and the ticking clock. But this time, I began thinking about this book, which was only about 25 percent written at that time. The events I had just gone through seemed to underscore an important message that I knew I had to include here—a call to all of my readers to think about what they considered to be the essence of a truly happy, successful life.

My wife returned later that afternoon to take me home. I had a complete follow-up physical with my regular doctor later that week, and I lost my driver's license until I passed a road test with the Department of Motor Vehicles, an inconsequential matter. I now had a whole new perspective on the importance of family, the true keys to success, and the secrets of living a more balanced, happy life. That perspective has shaped everything you've just read in this book.

Here's the important message I want to leave with you: You never know when your well-structured, organized, busy life might end!

As the second edition of this book goes to press in July, 2014, I'm most pleased to report that we've already heard from a number of you thanking us for writing *Peak Performance Under Pressure*. The problems, challenges, and disruptions of everyday life are painted with a broad brush. We all deal with them. Job titles, promotions, work success, and bonuses suddenly diminish compared with the loss of a loved one, a life-changing diagnosis, a debilitating illness, the break-up of a long-term relationship, or distressing addiction problems in the family. These major life events can tie us up in gut-wrenching knots—with no end in sight.

We are delighted to learn that some of our readers, dealing with these tough challenges, were able to more quickly re-balance their lives and regain their peace of mind based on the life-lessons of our book. To improve our focus, we have modified the title to *Peak Business Performance Under Pressure*.

One of my goals in writing this book has been to help you gain some insight into how *you* might live a happier, more balanced, and productive life. I believe that knowing how to deal with the pressures of work is essential to that effort, an idea based on a simple premise: *Less pressure = less stress = a more productive, more balanced, and happier you.*

The idea is simple, but acting on it can be tough. Many times at work, you can't help but worry about what you should be doing at home. Then at home, you switch to worrying about work. Your days are packed, with so much to do. You haven't exercised in a month—you've been too busy. You feel yourself getting wired tighter and tighter. There's no end in sight. You come home exhausted, and it's only Tuesday. You're too tired and worried about all that's on your plate to sleep well. You decide that next week you'll start eating better and go back to the gym. When Monday rolls around, it all begins again.

According to many psychologists, your work will always expand to match the amount of time you're willing to spend working. Who wants to become a stressed-out workaholic without a life? Your rationale is to tell yourself you need this job, or you need the money. Fair answers. But my point is that, no matter what, you need to keep your life balanced. Without a balanced approach to work and life, you risk trading your health to acquire wealth. All this frantic busy-ness could be costing you big time. Someday, sooner than you think, you may find yourself in one of those long, blurry ambulance rides—or pay an even more terrible price with your health. But it doesn't have to be that way.

I hope that you can use the techniques and tools I've outlined in this book to help you take better care of yourself at work, to get the most important things done first, to reduce your stress, to do your best and be your best, and to live a more balanced life. As difficult as this may sound, you can do it. And your first step is to get a better handle on your workplace pressures and find logical, practical ways to control them. That's what I hope you've found in the Peak Performance Formula and the many ideas for using it that I've shared with you.

Regardless of their profession—from CEOs, to senior executives, to department heads, to rising stars, to salespeople, to TOPGUN students—just about everyone I've ever worked with has shared the same goal: to live a happier, more productive, and balanced life. Use the ideas you've learned here to pursue that goal. Pick out one or two easy things you can implement right now. Then take action. Next week, pick out two more easy things and take action. Keep at it. Remember that foundation principle of the Aces: *The day you stop wanting to get better is the day you stop being good.*

It's been my sincere privilege to spend time with you on the pages of this book. We've covered a lot of emotional territory together. I wish you and your families a long and peaceful life. And to all in business, good luck and good hunting.

Bill Driscoll
U.S. Navy Ace

Bibliography and Suggested Reading

Burg, Bob, and John David Mann. *The Go-Giver: A Little Story About a Powerful Business Idea.* New York: Portfolio, 2007.

Carnegie, Dale. *How to Win Friends and Influence People.* New York: Simon & Schuster, 1937.

Claxton, Guy. *Hare Brain, Tortoise Mind: Why Intelligence Increases When You Think Less.* New York: HarperCollins, 1997.

Collins, Jim. *Good to Great: Why Some Companies Make the Leap . . . and Others Don't.* New York: HarperCollins, 2001.

Gallagher, Winifred. *Rapt: Attention and the Focused Life.* New York: Penguin Press, 2009.

Gladwell, Malcolm. *Blink: The Power of Thinking Without Thinking,* 1st ed. New York: Little, Brown, 2005.

Gladwell, Malcolm. *The Outliers: The Story of Success.* Boston: Little, Brown, 2008.

Gladwell, Malcolm. *The Tipping Point: How Little Things Can Make a Big Difference,* 1st ed. Boston: Little, Brown, 2000.

Goodwin, Doris Kearns. *Team of Rivals: The Political Genius of Abraham Lincoln.* New York: Simon & Schuster, 2005.

Harari, Oren. *The Leadership Secrets of Colin Powell,* 1st ed. New York: McGraw-Hill, 2002.

Sachs, Jeffrey. *Common Wealth: Economics for a Crowded Planet.* New York: Penguin Press, 2008.

Salter, James. *The Hunters.* New York: Vintage Books, 1997.

Toliver, Raymond F., and Trevor J. Constable. *The Blond Knight of Germany: A Biography of Erich Hartmann.* London: Parker, 1970.

Thurow, Lester. *Fortune Favors the Bold: What We Must Do to Build a New and Lasting Global Prosperity.* New York: HarperCollins, 2003.

Whitaker, Todd. *The Ball.* Bloomington, IN: Triple Nickel Press, 2010.

Zakaria, Fareed. *The Post-American World.* New York: Norton, 2008.

Index

About the Authors

Bill Driscoll flew 170 combat missions during the Vietnam War as a Radar Intercept Officer in the F-4 Phantom jet fighter. Over his forty-one-year career in U.S. Naval Aviation, he logged more than 3,300 hours of jet fighter flight time, made 500 aircraft carrier landings, and flew in more than 5,200 dogfights. Driscoll is one of only two Navy Vietnam War Aces with shoot-downs of five enemy jet fighters in aerial combat.

Driscoll was awarded the Navy's highest medal for valor, the Navy Cross, and was nominated for America's highest military decoration, the Medal of Honor. Among his many other awards are two Silver Stars, the Purple Heart, and ten Air Medals. His combat record makes him one of the most highly decorated living Naval Flight Officers of the past fifty years. He remains the youngest U.S. Navy Ace.

After twelve years of active duty, including four years as an instructor at the Navy's elite TOPGUN fighter weapons school, Driscoll transferred to the Navy Reserves. He has a forty-year association with TOPGUN. For the past twenty-three years, Driscoll has served as an air-combat consultant providing the four graduating TOPGUN classes each year with a candid three-hour, real-world air-combat presentation.

Driscoll also worked twenty-six years in the highly competitive field of commercial real estate for CB Richard Ellis in California's San Diego North County. Applying those lessons of peak pressure performance he had learned as an Ace and TOPGUN instructor, he earned the Number One Salesman award in his office five times. His 500 lease transactions totaled more than $200 million, and commercial land sales totaled approximately 645 acres and $145 million.

Since 1995, Driscoll has served as a business consultant for many major companies around the United States. He is in constant demand for his unique motivation and leadership presentations.

His remarkable experiences provide him with a matchless perspective on how to perform at a high level of effectiveness under maximum pressure. Driscoll has noted many times that Ace fighter pilots, top-performing senior and mid-level executives, highly effective sales staffs, and outstanding marketing personnel share much in common. All face ever-increasing pressures from rapidly expanding global competition, shifting markets, and an unprecedentedly challenging global economy. As he often notes, everyone in corporate America today is under increasingly intense pressure to accomplish more with less.

Driscoll earned a Bachelor of Arts in Economics from Stonehill College. He also has a Masters of Science in System Management from the University of Southern California. More information is available at www.willydriscoll.com.

Peter Joffre Nye is a prize-winning writer who worked thirty years in Washington, DC, as a journalist and magazine editor, wrote a documentary script, and authored six books. His articles have been published in more than 100 newspapers and magazines, including the *Washington Post, USA Today*, and *Sports Illustrated*. Since 1988, he has been a trustee of the U.S. Bicycling Hall of Fame. He studied at Ball State University and the London School of Economics, and received an MFA in Creative Nonfiction from Goucher College.

Books from Allworth Press

Allworth Press is an imprint of Skyhorse Publishing, Inc. Selected titles are listed below.

Brand Thinking and Other Noble Pursuits
by Debbie Millman (6 x 9, 320 pages, paperback, $19.95)

Building Design Strategy
by Thomas Lockwood and Thomas Walton (6 x 9, 272 pages, paperback, $24.95)

Corporate Creativity
by Thomas Lockwood and Thomas Walton (6 x 9, 256 pages, paperback, $24.95)

Design Thinking
by Thomas Lockwood (6 x 9, 304 pages, paperback, $24.95)

Emotional Branding, Revised Edition
by Marc Gobé (6 x 9, 344 pages, paperback, $19.95)

Infectious: How to Connect Deeply and Unleash the Energetic Leader Within
by Achim Nowak (6 x 9, 256 pages, paperback, $19.95)

Living Trusts for Everyone
by Ronald Farrington Sharp (5 ½ x 8 ½, 160 pages, paperback, $14.95)

The Pocket Small Business Owner's Guide to Building Your Business
by Kevin Devine (5 ½ x 8 ¼, 256 pages, paperback, $14.95)

The Pocket Small Business Owner's Guide to Business Plans
by Brian Hill and Dee Power (5 ½ x 8 ¼, 224 pages, paperback, $14.95)

The Pocket Small Business Owner's Guide to Negotiating
by Kevin Devine (5 ½ x 8 ¼, 224 pages, paperback, $14.95)

The Pocket Small Business Owner's Guide to Starting Your Business on a Shoestring
by Carol Tice (5 ½ x 8 ¼, 244 pages, paperback, $14.95)

The Pocket Small Business Owner's Guide to Taxes
by Brian Germer (5 ½ x 8 ¼, 240 pages, paperback, $14.95)

To see our complete catalog or to order online, please visit *www.allworth.com*